TROUBLED TO TREASURED

Strong Willed Child, or Strong Willed Parent?

FRANK M. ROMO

Order this book online at www.trafford.com
or email orders@trafford.com

Most Trafford titles are also available at major online book retailers.

Printed in Victoria, BC, Canada.

ISBN: 978-1-4269-0574-2 (sc)

Library of Congress Control Number: 2010906378

Our mission is to efficiently provide the world's finest, most comprehensive book publishing service, enabling every author to experience success. To find out how to publish your book, your way, and have it available worldwide, visit us online at www.trafford.com

Trafford rev. 08/03/2010

 www.trafford.com

North America & international
toll-free: 1 888 232 4444 (USA & Canada)
phone: 250 383 6864 ♦ fax: 812 355 4082

CONTENTS

INTRODUCTION

I recently attended a meeting, which supposedly was intended to help a youth who was having difficulty in school. He would not do his schoolwork and created disturbances in the classroom. By their own statements, the administrative staff admitted that they were at their wits' end regarding ways to motivate this child.

I've heard the same statements in similar meetings and from frustrated parents as well. In most of these cases, there were no apparent handicaps other than social skills; the children demonstrated the ability to achieve academically, but they simply wouldn't make an effort. In this case, as in others, the youth's behavior was seen as a means to get attention. They were demanding that he meet their expectations by using intimidating and coercive means. They expected him, a socially handicapped child, to understand all the ramifications of their positions when they weren't even able to recognize or understand them themselves. By their own statements they had failed to motivate him; they had failed to recognize his real needs, and were failing to teach him academic as well as associated social skills to enable him to meet their demands. They were "putting the cart before horse," so to speak and then blaming the child for their own failure.

In fact, *they* were reinforcing the very behavior they were trying to extinguish. But meeting the child's real needs must precede the response that *they* desire and that of society in general.

I don't mean to suggest that the many people working with children having these handicaps are ignorant or not sincerely interested in helping these children succeed, but they simply don't have the appropriate knowledge or the skills to achieve their ends. Those that do have the skills are, too often, misled by false assumptions that have no basis in fact; there is no conclusive empirical evidence to support those assumptions.

In working with these children for over forty years, I have repeatedly succeeded in bringing about changes in their lives—often dramatic changes. I have helped them function much better and achieve their potential interpersonal relationship skills. I've worked with some considered the most difficult of all. I've worked with them in nearly every possible social situation.

The data I offer is neither new nor original, merely presented from a different perspective and correlated into a single comprehensive statement. When adhered to, I have consistently achieved the desired results. This is not a matter of my personal evaluation, but a matter of public record, as well as the testimonies of parents, clients, co-workers, and administrators.

In efforts to communicate this information to those working with these children, I've found that too many reject any input that may change their position. The subject is too complex to simply explain "off the top of my head." Yet many of the parents I've spoken to can identify with what I say. They testify to my results, but they have also found difficulty being heard. When they attempt to communicate their knowledge of their child's idiosyncrasies, they find themselves being blamed for their child's behavior.

Those responsible for teaching the children blame the child for their own failings rather than question their methods. If a method isn't working, the only logical conclusion is to change the method. The purpose of this book is to present other methods based on empirical evidence and recorded results.

My primary focus is to present evidence to aid in the recognition of specific, identifiable personalities who have many symptoms ascribed to other personality types, but who have additional symptoms which, collectively, identify them as a specific personality type requiring special treatment techniques. The techniques and concepts to be presented are not new. They are being de-emphasized in favor of more popular methods. Too many of the popular methods are based on false assumptions without empirical evidence to support them. What support they do have is inconsistent and merely based on chance results, or inadvertently using appropriate techniques, unknowingly and haphazardly.

My original intention was to describe a specific personality and effective methods for treating them. However, as I proceeded with my work, I realized it would be necessary to describe other personality types and the specific effective methods for treating them. My purpose for doing this is to emphasize the need for differential treatment methods as suggested by the authors of the "I-Level Theory" and attempted at The California Youth Authority institution of O.H. Close School for Boys in Stockton, California, in 1963.

In the following chapters, I intend to present the findings and theories of others, ones I have utilized to justify my assumptions and techniques. These early chapters (Section I) may seem complex for the layman and many parents, but I hope to clarify these complexities in the latter chapters (Section II) dealing with treatment techniques. My repeated results provide evidence that my techniques are successful, though some of my rationale may be questionable. I do not profess to be the most knowledgeable person regarding the many aspects of the human organism; however, my results testify to my skill in changing the behavior of children often described as "monsters" to the most loving and lovable children I've encountered. I might add that this is not, nor is it intended to be, a scientific treatise. However, it can well suggest several areas that would be worth thoroughly researching.

Unfortunately, my references are limited, since I never intended to present a scientific article describing my work much less write a book about it. Many of the articles from which I gained my data were never recorded. In many instances, data I acquired was secondary data that I encountered while doing other research work. At the time, they appeared to be merely unrelated bits of information, but later were found to be significantly related.

It is hoped that the readers will judge my work by my results rather than my literary skills.

I

Theoretical Background

CHAPTER I

Diagnosis: An Introduction to I-Level Theory

Many social ills can best be attributed to lack of social skills. Inadequate interpersonal relationship skills are not being adequately addressed, nor are they even being identified, specifically. The general consensus in our society attributes these attitudes to ignorance due to various inappropriate teachings. The I Level Theory, described below, does address this condition, and quite specifically. The statement below, as well as further studies, strongly indicates a congenital disorder hinders certain identifiable persons, who, through no fault of their own, are totally incapable of comprehending the social mores of our society, within accepted limits.

We have found, however, that under certain given conditions they can learn to improve their skills to a more acceptable level, but never to the norm of their chronological age. They are unable to change their I-Level, their core personalities, nor their basic behavior patterns. (There have been some that have appeared to be exceptions, but these can be explained as simply the results of environmental changes, which enhance the learning opportunities for those with the genetic makeup for comprehending these teachings.)

Though the I-Level Theory focused on delinquent youths, I found through my field experiences, these same personalities exist throughout society. They represent a large population of persons who fit these types and whose lives are filled with problems, stemming from inadequate and inappropriate social skills. Their difficulties bring them to the attention of various agencies.

In the 1950s and 60s, a theory known as The I-Level Theory was developed. Though there remained much to be learned about the many possible ways this theory might be utilized, it did prove to be a very accurate classification system. It also provided the groundwork for the development of differential treatment.

While it was being used by the Parole Division of The California Youth Authority, I had an opportunity to develop a treatment program for a special unit of the CYA's Fricot Ranch School for Boys. This was a unit of twenty boys, between the ages of seven and twelve, considered to be the youngest and the most difficult children to work with.

In my previous assignment, we had implemented many therapeutic techniques still in the early stage of their development, and/or their experimental stage. During a training session with our Research Division, it was stated that 10% of our wards had a 90% recidivism rate in a six-month period. They did not meet the criteria for our program and, simply put, we didn't have a program for them.

At the time, most could be seen as society's rejects. Many parents didn't want them, neighbors didn't want them around, the police didn't want them on the streets, even juvenile halls didn't want them and the schools didn't want them. At the time, they didn't meet the criteria for The Department of Mental Health, so the only place available for them was the state's correctional facilities for youthful offenders.

In the following months, I attempted to identify the differences between those who succeeded and those who failed on parole, and also noted the differences in their involvement in the various activities available on the living units.

Through a promotional transfer, I was given the opportunity to further my efforts, and to develop a unique and innovative treatment plan for the "Pioneer Lodge" of Fricot Ranch School. The program was originally designed as a follow-up of Fritz Redl's (co-author of *The Aggressive Child*) Pioneer House in Detroit. The initial results were insignificant, according to reports of some of those who actively participated in the program. This was followed by a more intensive research project, which in turn was reported to have had little significant success.

Armed with my previous experiences and independent observations, I proposed a plan that I felt could be dedicated to that 10% with the 90% recidivism rate. At this point, it was noted that my proposed plan was very similar to that of the Community Treatment Project (CTP) of the CYA Parole Division. The Assistant Superintendent of Fricot and overseer of our program, Cal Terhune, suggested a meeting with their staff, which resulted in our incorporating the I-Level theory in our plan.

The results of our treatment plan, as reported by the Parole Division, was 17% recidivism in a 2½ year period. Due to the success of the plan, it was adapted to be the treatment plan for the CYA, O.H. Close School for Boys in Stockton, California.

The following is an introductory statement about the I-Level Theory written by Cal Terhune, Superintendent of O.H. Close School for Boys, as reprinted from the 1966 edition of *Interpersonal Maturity Level Classification: Juvenile Diagnosis and Treatment of Low, Middle and High Maturity Delinquents*, which was prepared by Marguerite Q. Warren and the Community Treatment Staff, Community Treatment Project, California Youth Authority:

Differential treatment is one of the primary goals of the 0. H. Close School. The Interpersonal Maturity Level (I-level) is the classification system that will be used.

This paper provides the latest material developed as related to juvenile delinquents. It provides descriptions of the theory, I-levels, sub-types, characteristics and treatment plans as developed by the staff of the Community Treatment Project.

All staff are urged to give careful study to this paper. It is not the final word on classification and treatment; it will undoubtedly be revised in the light of continued experiences. By understanding the basic theory, and testing some of the treatment suggestions, members of our Treatment Teams will be in a position to further the development of more effective treatment techniques.

The following text is the original evaluation, which is followed by revisions I've suggested. My suggestions are based on observations in controlled residential settings, in outreach programs, in the community, as well as in various social situations, over a period of thirty years. Many of the observations identify subtle contingencies that were difficult to identify without these opportunities. I've only included the I-2s and I-3s because they require specific techniques that I've found to be most effective in treating their unique characteristics. They do not benefit from insight therapy and traditional methods, as do the I-4s.

5

Here, then, is the relevant text in its entirety, with a view to providing the theoretical background necessary to understanding the point I wish to make through this book. What follows is the Introduction to the 1965 revision, *Interpersonal Maturity Level Classification: Juvenile Diagnosis of Middle Maturity (I.) Delinquents*:

In the field of delinquency, agreed-upon "facts" are few indeed. Perhaps one of these "facts" is that delinquents are not all alike—that they are different from each other in the reasons for their delinquency, in the expression of their delinquency, and in their capacity for change toward non-delinquent patterns.

Many past and current attempts at classification have been made. These typologies have been justified in terms of (1) an aid in understanding delinquency, (2) an aid in conceptualizing for research investigation, and (3) an aid in treatment programming and case management for the administrator and practitioner.

It is particularly with the last of these—the treatment-control planning—in mind that the "Interpersonal Maturity Level Classification: Juvenile" scheme has been developed. This typology is an elaboration of the Sullivan, Grant and Grant Levels of Interpersonal Maturity, a theoretical formulation describing a sequence of personality integrations in normal childhood development. This classification system focuses upon the ways in which the delinquent is able to see himself and the world, especially in terms of emotions and motivations; i.e., his ability to understand what is happening between himself and others as well as between others.

Theoretical Frame of Reference

Seven successive stages of interpersonal maturity characterize psychological development. They range from the least mature, which resembles the interpersonal interactions of a newborn infant, to an ideal of social maturity, which is seldom, or never reached in our present culture. Each of the seven stages or levels is defined by a crucial interpersonal problem, which must be solved before further progress toward maturity can occur. All persons do not necessarily work their way through each stage but may become fixed at a particular level.[1] (1) The range of maturity levels found in a delinquent population is from Maturity Level 2 (Integration Level 2 or I-2) to Maturity Level 5 (I-5). Level 5 is infrequent enough that, for all practical purposes, use of levels 2 through 4 describes the juvenile population. A brief description of these levels follows:

Maturity Level 2 (I-2): The individual whose interpersonal understanding and behavior are integrated at this level is primarily involved with demands that the world take care of him. He sees others primarily as "givers" or "withholders" and has no conception of interpersonal refinement beyond this. He is unable to explain, understand or predict the behavior or reactions of others. He is not interested in things outside himself except as a source of supply. He behaves impulsively, unaware of the effects of his behavior on others.

Maturity Level 3 (I-3): The individual who operates at this level is attempting to manipulate his environment in order to get what he wants. In contrast to level 2, he is at least aware that his own behavior has something to do with whether or not he gets what he wants. He still does not differentiate, however, among people except to the extent that they can or cannot be useful to him.

He sees people only as objects to be manipulated in order to get what he wants. His manipulations may take the forms either of conforming to the rules of whoever seems to have the power at the moment ("If you can't lick them, join them.") or of the type of maneuvering characteristic of a "confidence man" ("Make a sucker out of him before he makes a sucker out of you."). He tends to deny having disturbing feelings or strong emotional involvement in his relationships with others.

Maturity Level 4 (I-4): An individual whose understanding and behavior are integrated at this level has internalized a set of standards by which he judges his and others' behavior. He is aware of the influence of others on him and their expectations of him. To a certain extent, he is aware of the effects of his own behavior on others. He wants to be like the people he admires. He may feel guilty about not measuring up to his internalized standards. If so, conflict produced by the feelings of inadequacy and guilt may be internalized with consequent neurotic symptoms or acted out in antisocial behavior. Instead of guilt over self worth, he may feel conflict over values. Or, without conflict, he may admire and identify with delinquent models, internalizing their delinquent values.

It should be stressed that interpersonal development is viewed as a continuum. The successive steps or levels, which are described in this theory, are seen as definable points along the continuum. As such, they represent "ideal types." Individuals are not classified at the level which reflects their maximum capabilities under conditions of extreme comfort, but rather are categorized at that level which represents their typical level, of functioning or, their capacity to function, under conditions of stress. This rating of basal level has the advantage of permitting more accurate predictions of behavior in a delinquent population.

Nine Delinquent Subtypes

In 1961, an elaboration of the Maturity Level Classification was developed for use in the Community Treatment Project. In part, the elaboration was drawn from the work of the California Youth Authority Committee on Standard Nomenclature in an effort to describe more specifically the juvenile population.

The "Interpersonal Maturity Level Classification: Juvenile" subdivided the three major types described above into nine delinquent subtypes, as follows:

Code Name Delinquent Subtype

I-2 Aa	Unsocialized	Aggressive	"demanding"
Ap	Unsocialized	Passive	"complaining"
I-3 Cfm	Conformist	immature	"conforming"
Cfc	Conformist	Cultural	"conforming"
Mp	Manipulator		"manipulating"
I-4 Na	Neurotic	Acting-out	"defending"
NX	Neurotic	Anxious	"defending"
Ci	Cultural Identifier	"identifying"	
Se	Situational Emotional Reaction	"identifying"	

Whereas the Maturity Level classification represented a categorization of the individual's level of perceptual differentiation, the subtype represented a categorization of the individual's response to his view of the world.

The nine subtypes then were described by lists of item definitions, which characterized the manner in which each group perceived the world, responded to the world, and were perceived by others.

Differential Treatment Planning

As noted earlier, the major reason for the elaboration of the Maturity Level Classification was the need to develop rational treatment-control procedures for different types of delinquents in the Community Treatment Program. Therefore, the 1961 classification manual also included preliminary suggestions for the handling of the various subtypes.

The early treatment plans were considered educated guesses. The treatment suggestions were not completely arm-chaired but were based to some extent on findings about interaction between delinquent type and treatment type emerging from several clinical and experimental studies. However, it was assumed that the appropriateness and usefulness of the typology would have to be determined in the community setting, and that the treatment plans would have to be further specified, with their effectiveness tested and revisions made.

After four-and-a-half years of operation in the Community Treatment Project, the typology appears quite satisfactory—inclusive, reliable, and very useful in developing treatment strategies. As a result of our experience, item definitions describing the various subtypes have been revised and further elaborated. Treatment strategies have been further specified and, in a few instances, revised. It is hoped that the new definitions will facilitate diagnosis and treatment planning on the part of those attempting to use the classification system and treatment models. Perhaps even more important than the new definitions is the fact that the scheme can now be regarded as one which has withstood an operational test in the field.

My Comments

The theory suggests that there is a "continuum of steps" that must be achieved before progress toward the next level can occur. Some people become fixed at a particular level. This assumption, I believe, is somewhat erroneous. I have observed I-2s and I-3s for many years. Through various roles I've played in the community, I was able to observe them in different social environments, from different socio-economic backgrounds, with ages ranging from infants to seniors, of different intellects, and in different geographical locations. I worked with them in controlled residential settings, in outreach work, as a behavioral and insight therapist, as a landlord, and as a friend when they were residents in my home.

I've concluded that each level has its own continuum and the description is of their optimum level of achievement. I believe their inability to change I-Levels is genetically determined. I-2s and I-3s are the progeny of I-3 Mps. I've been able to trace the genealogies back as far as four generations of the biological Mp parent and I've yet to find any that doesn't fit the description specifically. Initially, it is sometimes difficult to make an accurate diagnosis, since when comfortable they can appear to be more insightful and more amiable. Though they can verbalize some mature insightful conclusions, they are unable to internalize what they learn and, consequently, cannot integrate it into their personalities.

I believe the I-Level Theory descriptions actually identify the maximum potential of each type. I believe each type has its own continuum to progress through to reach that potential. In observing young children of comparable chronological ages, I believe I've been able to identify and predict the potential of many children. Where I've been able to obtain follow-up data several years later, I found those predictions to be accurate.

As with other developmental tasks, not all children can reach the same degree of proficiency in completing those tasks. The I-Level Theory describes the degree of proficiency obtainable for each type. As with other developmental tasks, genetic factors play a role in determining the degree of success a child may achieve.

Notes and references for the quoted material in chapter 1

[1] Redl, Fritz & David Wineman. *The Aggressive Child.* The Free Press, Glencoe, Illinois, 1957.

[2] Warren, Marguerite Q. and the Community Treatment Staff, Community Treatment Staff, Community Treatment Project, California Youth Authority. The Development of Interpersonal Maturity: Applications to Delinquency. *Psychiatry*, 1957, 20, 373-385.

CHAPTER 2

Transactional Analysis

As I have mentioned, the data I'm presenting in these chapters are the results of the work of many others, as quoted from various sources. This data is not recent, but in view of their tested results are as relevant today as they were at the time of their reports.

For this chapter, I've chosen to use excerpts from Eric Berne's book, *Transactional Analysis In Psychotherapy*. In Chapter 8 of his book, Berne presents a depiction of the primary needs of the human organism and their influences on social intercourse. It is on these needs that he builds his theory of Transactional Analysis.

And it was on these needs that I built my reinforcement techniques for reshaping behavior. Here, then, is Berne's Chapter 8 on social intercourse. He begins with a discussion of the theory of social contact:

1 A Theory of Social Contract
The ability of the human psyche to maintain coherent ego states seems to depend upon a changing flow of sensory stimuli. This observation forms the psychobiological basis of social psychiatry. In structural

terms, these stimuli are necessary in order to assure the integrity of the neopsyche and the archaeopsyche. If the flow is cut off or flattened into monotony, it is observed that the neopsyche gradually becomes disorganized ("The individual's thinking is impaired"); this lays bare the underlying archaeopsychic activity ("He shows childish emotional responses"); and finally archaeopsychic function becomes disorganized as well ("He suffers from hallucinations"). This is the sensory deprivation experiment.

The work of Spitz goes a little farther. It demonstrates that sensory deprivation in the infant may result not only in psychic changes, but also in organic deterioration. This shows how vital it is for the changing sensory environment to be maintained. In addition, a new and specific factor appears: the most essential and effective forms of sensory stimulation are provided by social handling and physical intimacy. Hence Spitz speaks of "emotional deprivation" rather than of "sensory deprivation". The intolerance for long periods of boredom or isolation gives rise to the concept of stimulus-hunger, particularly for the kind of stimuli offered by physical intimacy. This stimulus-hunger parallels in many ways, biologically, psychologically, and socially, the hunger for food. Such terms as malnutrition, satiation, gourmet, gourmand, faddist, ascetic, culinary arts, and good cook are easily transferred from the field of nutrition to their analogues in the field of sensation. Overstuffing has its parallel in over-stimulation, which may cause difficulties by flooding the psyche with stimuli faster than they can be comfortably handled. In both spheres, under ordinary conditions where ample supplies are available and a diversified menu is possible, choices will be heavily influenced by individual idiosyncrasies.

The question of constitutional determinants of stimulation choices is not of present moment. Those idiosyncrasies which are of immediate interest to the social psychiatrist are based on archaic experiences, neopsychic judgments, and particularly in regard to physical intimacy, exteropsychic prejudices. These introduce varying amounts of caution, prudence, and deviousness into the situation, so that eventually it is only under special circumstances that the individual will make a direct gesture toward the most prized forms of stimulation represented by physical relationships. Under most conditions he will compromise. He learns to do with more subtle, even symbolic forms of handling, until the merest nod of recognition may serve the purpose to some extent, although his original craving for physical contact may remain unabated. As the complexities increase, each person becomes more and more individual in his quest, and it is these differentia which lend variety to social intercourse.

The stimulus-hunger, with its first order sublimation into recognition-hunger, is so pervasive that the symbols of recognition become highly prized and are expected to be exchanged at every meeting between people. Deliberately withholding them constitutes a form of misbehavior called rudeness, and repeated rudeness is considered a justification for imposing social or even physical sanctions. The spontaneous forms of recognition, such as the glad smile, are most gratefully received. Other gestures, like the hiss, the obeisance, and the handshake, tend to become ritualized. In this country there is a succession of verbal gestures, each step implying more and more recognition and giving more and more gratification. This ritual may be typically summarized as follows: (a) "Hello!" (b) "How are you?" (c) "Warm enough for you?" (d) "What's new?" (e) "What else is new?" The implications are: (a) Someone is there; (b) Someone with feelings is there; (c) Someone with feelings and sensations is there; (d) Someone with feelings, sensations, and a personality is there; (e) Someone with feelings, sensations, a personality, and in whom I have more than a passing interest, is there.

A great deal of linguistic, social, and cultural structure revolves around the question of mere recognition: special pronouns, inflections, gestures, postures, gifts, and offerings are designed to exhibit recognition of status and person. The movie fan-letter is one of our indigenous products, which enables recognition to be depersonalized and quantified on an adding machine; and the difference between the printed mimeographed, photographic, and personal reply is something like the difference between the various steps of the greeting ritual described above. The unsatisfactory nature of such mechanical recognition is shown by the preference of many actors and actresses for the live theatre over the movies, even at a considerable financial sacrifice. This is a dramatic example of the extended validity of Spitz's principle.

2 The Structuring of Time

Mere recognition, however, is not enough, since after the rituals have been exhausted, tension mounts and anxiety begins to appear. The real problem of social intercourse is what happens after the rituals. Hence it is possible to speak not only of stimulus-hunger and social hunger, but also of structure-hunger. The everyday problem of the human being is the structure of his waking hours. If they are not structured for him, as they tend to be in infancy, then he is impelled to find or set up a structure independently, hour by hour.

The most common, convenient, comfortable, and utilitarian method of structuring time is by a project designed to deal with the material of external reality: what is commonly known as work. Such a project is technically called an activity; the term "work" is unsuitable because a general theory of social psychiatry must recognize that social inter-course is also a form of work.

Activities are of interest here only insofar as they offer a matrix for recognition and other more complex forms of social intercourse specific social problem takes the form of (1) how to structure time (2) here and now (3) most profitably on the basis of (4) one's own idiosyncrasies, (5) the idiosyncrasies of other people, and (6) the estimated potentialities of the immediate and eventual situations. The profit lies in obtaining the maximum of permissible satisfactions.

The operational aspect of time structuring may be called programming. Programming is supplied by three sources: material, social, and individual. Material programming arises from the vicissitudes encountered in dealing with external reality, and does not concern us here. Social programming has already been referred to in discussing greeting rituals. This is carried farther in what may be called pastimes, which generally take the form of semi-ritualistic discussions of common-places such as the weather, possessions, current events, or family affairs.

As people become less guarded, more and more individual programming creeps in, so that "incidents" begin to occur. These incidents superficially appear to be adventitious, and may be so described by the parties concerned, but careful scrutiny reveals that they tend to follow definite patterns which are amenable to sorting and classification, and that the sequence is in effect circumscribed by unspoken rules and regulations. These regulations remain latent as long as the amities or hostilities proceed according to Hoyle, but they become manifest if an illegal move is made, giving rise to a symbolic cry of "Foul!" Such sequences, which in contrast to pastimes are based more on individual than on social programming, may be called games. Family life and married life may be centered year after year around variations of the same game.

Pastimes and games are substitutes for the real living of real intimacy. Because of this they may be regarded as preliminary engagements rather than as unions; in effect, they are poignant forms of play.

When individual, usually instinctual, programming becomes more intense, both social patterning and ulterior restrictions begin to give way. This condition may be denoted crasis, a genuine interlocking of personalities; or more colloquially, it may be called intimacy.

Thus social contact, whether or not it is embedded in a matrix of activity, may be said to take two forms: play and intimacy. By far the greater part of all social intercourse is in the form of play.

3 Social Intercourse

The overt manifestations of social intercourse are called transactions. Typically these occur in chains: a transactional stimulus from X elicits a transactional response from Y; this response becomes a stimulus for X, and X's response in turn becomes a new stimulus for Y. Transactional Analysis is concerned with the analysis of such chains. and particularly with their programming. It can be demonstrated that once a chain is initiated, the resulting sequence is highly predictable if the characteristics of the Parent, Adult, and Child of each of the parties concerned is known. In certain cases, as will be shown later, the converse is also possible: given the initial transactional stimulus and the initial transactional response. not only the ensuing sequence, but also some of the characteristics of the Parent, Adult, and Child of each of the parties concerned can be deduced with a considerable degree of confidence.

While any type of social intercourse is amenable to transactional analysis, the transactional therapy group is especially designed to elicit the maximum amount of information concerning the idiosyncratic programming of each patient, since this programming is closely related to his symptomatology and also, barring accidents, determines his destiny. The characteristics of such a group are as follows:

1. Since there is no formal activity and no stated procedures, there's no external source of structuring for the time interval. Hence all programming is narrowed down to an interplay between that provided by the culture and that determined by previous special conditioning of the individual.

2. The commitment is only partial, and withdrawal of a given response, or withdrawal of the patient from the group, is possible without sanctions. The responsibilities are rarely as serious or permanent as those involved in such activities as bridge-building, or in such intimacies as impregnation. In these two respects to

group is similar to a social gathering such as a cocktail party. But it is distinguished by the following two criteria:

3. There is, however, a definite commitment to decisive group structure. The therapist is in one region and the patients in the other, and this is irreversible. The patients pay the therapist or follow the rules of his clinic, but the therapist never pays the patients. (So far, at least not in his capacity as therapist.)

4. The population for which the group is drawn is not of the patient's choosing, although he may sometimes have the privilege of selecting or rejecting members from the population of candidates. In the two latter respects the therapy group resembles many activity groups which have a ready-made program, such as business or educational institutions, but is differentiated by the first two criteria.

Notes
Structure-hunger. The experimentalists state quite explicitly and it is not merely a quantitative sensory deprivation that causes the disorganization, but some defect in structuring, a "monotony" which gives rise to "boredom". The classical illustration is offered by the struggles of Robinson Crusoe to ward off his oral confusion by structuring time and place on his solitary island. Crusoe exemplifies poignantly not only structure hunger but also social hunger. The accuracy of this fictional portrait is impressively shown by the experiences of forced isolates in real life: Baron Trenk during his 10 years in Magdeburg, Casanova during his confinement in the Leads in Venice, and John Bunyan during his 12 years in the county jail at Bedford. The cathectic drainage of the neopsyche caused by stimulus, social, and structure deprivation can be demonstrated by comparing patients in good state hospitals with those in bad state hospitals. The archaic suggestibility which results from such deprivation has apparently proven to be one of the most powerful weapons available to ruthless leaders in dealing with intransigent personalities.

Play. Play does not necessarily mean "kidding". In fact most human play, as Huizinga makes clear, is accompanied by genuine emotional intensity. This can be observed at any college campus or card-room. The essential point of social play in humans is not that the emotions are spurious, but that they are regulated. This is revealed when sanctions are imposed on an illegitimate emotional display. Thus play may be deadly serious, or even fatally serious, but the social consequences are only serious if the rules are abrogated.

For a discussion of the contract "this is play," see Bateson et al. In human beings, the conscious contract "This is play" often conceals an unconscious contract "This is not play." A variation of this is the true word which is spoken in jest, for which the speaker cannot be held responsible providing he smiled when he said it. Similarly the conscious contract "This is not play" (e.g., the marriage contract) may conceal a covert or unconscious contract "This is play." A good example of this is the game of "Frigid Woman," with its complex but orderly sequence of mutual provocations and recriminations. The overt contract implies a serious sexual union, but the covert contract says: "Don't take my sexual promises seriously." The same applies to the game of "Debtor" occasionally played by certain types of psychiatric patients in regard to money matters. Jackson and Weakland give a verbatim report away from the present one in view is a sinister game called "Double Bind" played by "schizophrenic families".

It is interesting to note that the findings of modern psychological research and the ideas expressed in this chapter although arriving at by quite a different route, are similar to some of Kierkegaard's reflections on boredom (1843). In addition, social control, the behavioral goal of transactional analysis, results in just the kind of optional apartness that Kierkegaard seemed to have in mind when he discusses such relationships as friendship marriage, and business. The concept of a slight but significant apartness is opposed to the pressure for "togetherness" that is active on both sides nowadays.

In the extreme position, it may be said that there might be small quarrels, but there could be no wars if people did not come together in groups. This is hardly a practical solution, but it is a good starting point for meditations about war and peace.

Notes and references for the quoted material in chapter 2

1. Heron, W. "The Pathology of Boredom". Scientific American 196: 52-56, January, 1957
2. Spitz, R. "Hospitalism, Genesis of Psychiatric Conditions in Early Childhood." Psychoanalytic study of the child. 1: 53-74, 1945.
3. Berne, E. "The Psychological Structure of Space with Some Remarks on the Robinson Crusoe," Psychoanalytic Quart. 25: 549-567, 1956
4. Huizinga, J. Homo Ludens, Beacon Press, Boston, 1955.
5. Bateson, G., et. al. "The Message "This is Play"." Transactions of Second Conference on Group Processes. Josiah Macy, Jr. Foundation, New York, 1956.
6. Weakland, J. H. & Jackson D. D. "Observations on a Schizophrenic Episode" Arch. Neur. & Psych. 79: 554-574, 1958.
7. Kierkegaard, S. A Kierkegaard Anthology, ed. R. Bretall. Princeton University Press Princeton, 1947. pp. 22 ff.

CHAPTER 3

Gestalt Therapy: An Introduction

In his introduction to Gestalt Therapy1, Gary Yontef states:

> Gestalt therapy is a phenomenological-existential
> therapy founded by Frederick (Fritz) and
> Laura Perls in the 1940s. It teaches therapists
> and patients the phenomenological method of
> awareness, in which perceiving, feeling, and
> acting are distinguished from interpreting and
> reshuffling pre-existing attitudes. Explanations
> and interpretations are considered less reliable
> than what is directly perceived and felt. Patients
> and therapists in Gestalt therapy dialogue,
> that is, communicate their phenomenological
> perspectives. Differences in perspectives become
> the focus of experimentation and continued
> dialogue. The goal is for clients to become aware
> of what they are doing, how they are doing it, and
> how they can change themselves, and at the same
> time, to learn to accept and value themselves.

Also:

> Gestalt therapy can be used effectively with any patient population that the therapist understands and feels comfortable with. If the therapist can relate to the patient, the Gestalt therapy principles of dialogue and direct experiencing can be applied. With each patient, general principles must be adapted to the particular clinical situation. If the patient's treatment is made to conform to "Gestalt therapy," it can be ineffective or harmful. A schizophrenic, a sociopath, a borderline and an obsessive-compulsive neurotic may all need different approaches. Thus, the competent practice of Gestalt therapy requires a background in more than Gestalt therapy. A knowledge of diagnosis, personality theory and psychodynamic theory is also needed.

And:

> Another difference from other therapies is Gestalt therapy's genuine regard for holism and multidimensionality. People manifest their distress in how they behave, think and feel. "Gestalt therapy views the entire biopsychosocial field, including organism/environment, as important. Gestalt therapy actively uses physiological, sociological, cognitive, motivational variables. No relevant dimension is excluded in the basic theory.

As will be pointed out in the section of Treatment Strategies, awareness is my same goal as that of the Gestalt Therapist; however, for the particular personalities that this paper focuses on, certain preliminary therapies are essential for them to reach a point where they are amenable to Gestalt Therapy, per se. Depending on your perspective, the methods used do not necessarily follow prescribed Gestalt techniques. Here again, as Yontef points out, "Gestalt therapists may use any techniques or methods as long as (a) they are aimed toward increasing awareness, (b) they emerge out of dialogue and phenomenologic work, and (c) they are within the parameters of ethical practice."

Yontef also notes:

> The theoretical distinction between Gestalt
> therapy, behavior modification and psychoanalysis
> is clear. In behavior modification, the patient's
> behavior is directly changed by the therapist's
> manipulation of environmental stimuli. In
> psychoanalytic theory, behavior is caused
> by unconscious motivation which becomes
> manifest in the transference relationship. By
> analyzing the transference the repression is
> lifted, the unconscious becomes conscious. In
> Gestalt therapy, the patient learns to fully use
> his internal and external senses so he can be self-
> responsible and self-supportive. Gestalt therapy
> helps the patient regain the key to this state, the
> awareness of the process of awareness. Behavior
> modification conditions [by] using stimulus
> control, psychoanalysis cures by talking about
> and discovering the cause of mental illness
> [the problem], and Gestalt therapy brings self-
> realization through here-and-now experiments in
> directed awareness.

As Yontef states:

> Gestalt therapy is most useful for patients open
> to working on self-awareness and for those
> who want natural mastery of their awareness
> process. Although some people claim they are
> interested in changing their behavior, most people
> seeking psychotherapy mainly want relief from
> discomfort. Their complaint may be generalized
> malaise, specific discomforts, or dissatisfaction in
> relationships. Patients often expect that relief will
> result from their therapist's doing the work rather
> than from their own efforts.

Furthermore, he says:

> Psychotherapy is most appropriate for persons
> who create anxiety, depression, and so forth
> by rejecting themselves, alienating aspects of
> themselves, and deceiving themselves. In short,
> people who do not know how they further their
> own unhappiness are prime candidates, providing
> they are open to awareness work, especially
> awareness of self-regulation. Gestalt therapy
> is especially appropriate for those who know
> intellectually about themselves and yet don't grow.

And finally,

> Those who want symptom relief without doing
> awareness work may be better candidates for
> behavior modification, medication, biofeedback,

and so on. The direct methods of Gestalt therapy facilitate patients' making this choice early in the therapy. However, patients' difficulty in doing the contact or awareness work should not automatically be interpreted as meaning that they do not want to work.

Respect for the total person enables a Gestalt therapist to help the patients become clear about the differences between "can't" and "won't" and to know how internal barriers or resistance, such as prior learning, anxiety, shame and sensitivity to narcissistic injury, inhibit awareness work.

My Comments

The goal of my early work was to turn delinquent youths into non-delinquents. We had a time factor to work with as prescribed by the CYA. Later, in the field, time and opportunity were factors. My ultimate goal was to help dysfunctional people become functional by improving their social skills so that they were better able to function reasonably well in society. This entailed increasing their awareness of their social and physical environment, and their relationship to it. In essence, these are principles of Gestalt Therapy.

Notes for chapter 3

[1] Originally, when I began writing this book many years ago, my source for the following Yontef quotes was an edition that I no longer have in my possession, or at my disposal. However, Yontef's "Introduction to Gestalt" was later incorporated into *Awareness, Dialogue, and Process* published by The Gestalt Journal Press and copyrighted in 1993. This publication is cited in the list of sources, and permissions have been granted for that edition.

For more information concerning Yontef's Introduction to Gestalt Therapy and/or Gestalt Therapy in general, please visit the following website: http://www.gestalt.org/yontef.htm.

CHAPTER 4

Operant Conditioning: Skinner

Psychology is an extensively broad subject. There have been many studies done to isolate some of these aspects through scientific methods. Many of these studies, though not conclusive in themselves, identify areas that require more control to achieve their goals. The goal of science as described by Skinner is: "prediction, control, and interpretation." Skinner hoped to achieve this on the basis of his clinical studies. He was able to draw certain conclusions from these studies.

The following is a summary of many of those conclusions presented in his and Holland's book, *The Analysis of Behavior, A Program for Self-Instruction*. I'm presenting those that I believed to be significant in my assumptions and applications.

This is not a complete summary of the book—these are verbatim quotations. I have not paraphrased nor edited them. My hope is that this list may act as a "glossary" for defining my methods and will be referred to as I describe my message in my chapter on applications:

Reflex Behavior:

1. If the presentation of a stimulus is the "cause" of a response. The two form a reflex. In a reflex, a stimulus always precedes a response.

2. The magnitude of a stimulus is the intensity which is barely sufficient to elicit a response. In a reflex, the magnitude of the response varies with the magnitude of the stimulus. The more intense the stimulus the greater the magnitude of the response and the shorter the latency of reflex.

3. In reflex behavior, a process by which a new stimulus comes to elicit a response is called conditioning. A process by which a stimulus loses the power to elicit a response is called extinction.

4. An important aspect of the conditioning procedure is the time between presentation of the initially neutral stimulus and of the unconditioned stimulus. The interval between the stimulus to be conditioned and the unconditioned stimulus must be rather short.

5. Types of response mechanisms:
   a. Contractions of the striated or striped muscles (so-called because of their appearance under a microscope) move parts of the skeletal frames, as well as certain "flaps" of tissues such as the tongue, eyelid, and vocal cords.
   b. Glands secrete fluids into ducts or directly into the bloodstream.
   c. Responses of smooth muscles and glands are elicited by appropriate stimuli. They are response mechanisms in the stimulus-response relations termed reflexes.

d. The type of response mechanism usually involved in the organism's action upon the external environment are the striated muscles.

e. Most of the behavior which acts upon the external environment is not elicited by stimuli in the form of simple reflexes. That is to say, eliciting stimuli are not the principal "causes" of the responses executed by striated muscle.

f. In some cases, as in the flexion reflex, responses by striated muscles are elicited by stimuli, but most responses of striated muscles are not under the control of the eliciting stimuli.

g. The internal economy of the body depends on the secretion of digestive juices and on forcing substances through tubular organs by rhythmic changes in their diameters. The internal economy depends on the action of smooth muscles and glands.

Operant Conditioning:

6. Food is not reinforcing unless the animal has first been deprived of food for some time. Food is probably not reinforcing if the animal is not hungry.

7. When a response has been reinforced, it will be emitted more frequently in the future.

8. Because the response does not appear to be produced by an eliciting stimulus, it is said to be emitted. This type of behavior which operates or acts on the environment is called Operant Behavior.

9. Both positive and negative reinforcement increases the rate of response. Reinforcement which consists of presenting stimuli (e.g. food) is called positive reinforcement. In contrast, reinforcement which consists

of terminating stimuli (e.g., painful stimuli) is called negative reinforcement.

10. Two ways of effectively preventing unwanted conditioned behavior are: to (1) extinguish it by withholding reinforcement and (2) to condition some incompatible behavior.

Tantrums:

11. The receipt of candy as a result of "throwing a tantrum" is an example of positive reinforcement. When the mother placates the child with candy and the child ceases to scream, both mother and child are, perhaps unknowingly, reinforcing each other's behavior. If termination of a temper tantrum reinforces a mother's response of giving candy to her child, the cessation of noise is an example of negative reinforcement. To avoid conditioning temper tantrums, the mother should not reinforce such behavior when it is emitted. If temper tantrums have been previously condition, the mother can extinguish the response by consistently not reinforcing it. When a temper tantrum results in the receipt of candy, the probability that the child will have a tantrum in the future increases. In addition to extinguishing temper tantrums, a mother may frequently reinforce "playing quietly." This would help to eliminate the tantrums by conditioning behavior which is incompatible with them.

Conditioned Reinforcers:

12. A reinforcer which is not dependent on any one specific deprivation is called a generalized reinforcer. A conditioned reinforcer becomes a generalized reinforcer when paired with many unconditioned reinforcers.

13. People frequently show approval just before they provide many different types of reinforcers. Smiles the word "good" and other "signs of approval" each an unconditioned generalized reinforcer.

14. You may show affection or approval to reinforce the response you want another person to emit more frequently.

15. You may withhold affection or approval to extinguish behavior you don't want another person to emit.

16. A conditioned reinforcer which has acquired its capacity to reinforce by being paired with food is effective only when the animal is hungry.

17. A parent "pays attention" when he approaches a child, looks at him, touches him, etc. these activities generate stimuli affecting the child. The parent also provides food, water or, loving care or, etc. The stimuli arising from the parental "attention" become (conditioned) generalized reinforcers for the child.

Speed of Conditioning:

18. Pigeon C's record does not reveal the speed of acquiring a key pecking response because other processes are also involved. The pigeon must first adapt to the box and click conditioning can occur very fast when adaptation is already completed and when each response is immediately reinforced.

Principles of Shaping New Behavior:

19. There are two aspects in shaping skillful behavior: (a) reinforcing only certain responses, which is called (1)

differential reinforcement; and (b) gradually raising the requirement for reinforcement, which is called (2) successive approximations.

20. It is more than simple conditioning when we differentially reinforce successive approximations to a final form of behavior. When you follow the procedure we are said to be shaping behavior.

21. For best results in shaping behavior, a conditioned reinforcer should be presented in a close temporal relation to the response.

Schedules Defined:

22. When an Operant is only occasionally followed by reinforcement the schedule of reinforcement is said to be intermittent.

23. A mother trying to stop temper tantrums may not have always given in to them.

24. Occasionally, when she is especially tired, she may. She is reinforcing temper tantrums intermittently. By intermittently reinforcing temper tantrums, the mother is making them very resistant to extinction.

25. In the early conditioning of a response, reinforcement must be rather frequent (preferably continuous); if this is not the case the response may be extinguished before the next reinforcement is due.

26. Responses reinforced by the generalized reinforcers of affection, approval, etc., often are extinguished very slowly because the subtlety of the stimuli has made the schedule intermittent.

Stimulus Generalization:

27. In the behavioral development of a child, smiles mark occasions for reinforcement.

28. The extent of the generalizations among the smiling and other facial expressions decreases as discriminations are developed.

29. The stimulus which closely precedes or accompanies in reinforced response acquires control over that response. The stimulus becomes an SD for the response

Chaining:

30. Each stimulus in each chain has the dual function of reinforcing the response it follows and being an SD for the response it precedes. In a chain of behavior, the same stimulus is both an SD and a reinforcing stimulus.

31. A stimulus will become an SD when a response which regularly follows it is reinforced. An SD will become a conditioned reinforcer when reinforcement regularly follows it closely in time.

Deprivation:

32. Deprivation is a procedure which in general increases the probability of a group of responses. The probability of food related behavior occurring is increased by food deprivation.

33. That figure shows that their rate of responding declines as the degree of deprivation declines.

34. A generalized reinforcer is not dependent upon one particular condition of deprivation.

35. Eating, drinking, sexual behavior, sleeping, and general activity all show cyclical changes when the various conditions of deprivation are not manipulated experimentally.

Activation Syndrome:

36. In the activation syndrome, the hormone called adrenaline releases sugar into the blood from the liver. In fear or anger, secretion of adrenaline is elicited from the adrenal gland. In the activation syndrome, the blood is richly supplied with sugar and oxygen which are carried to muscle tissue more quickly by the increased pulse rate. In strong emotion the eyes bulge slightly, and the pupils dilate (enlarge). The respondents allow more light to enter the eye. The activation syndrome is biologically useful if great physical exertion is required (as in running or fighting). Strong emotional responses after a heavy meal may be harmful because, in the activation syndrome, gastric secretion ceases, and contractions of the stomach and intestines cease. A painful or frightening stimulus elicits many responses as part of the respondent behavior seen in the emotions of fear or anger.

37. While the activation syndrome always occurs in fear, anger, anxiety, etc., it also occurs as a result of heavy work in the absence of emotion. Hence the activation syndrome does not necessarily imply emotion.

Predispositions in Emotion:

38. Words like "bad" and "wrong" frequently accompany punishment. Therefore, through conditioning, the

words come to elicit the respondents of the activation syndrome.

39. Deprivation known conditions alter the probability of a whole class of responses. Similarly, emotional conditions alter the probability of a whole class of responses.

40. A hungry animal can be reinforced with food; a frightened animal can be reinforced by termination of the threatening condition.

41. Even when deprived of food, an anxious person may not eat. The responses which increase in probability during anxiety are incompatible with eating.

42. Physical restraint is an unconditioned emotional stimulus for infants; thus it elicits the reflex responses of the activation syndrome.

43. Physical restraint, an unconditioned emotional stimulus for an infant, elicits emotional behavior of the activation syndrome, and provides for the reinforcement of any operant behavior which removes the restraint.

Avoidance and Escape Behavior:

44. The emotional predisposition called anxiety is generated by Conditioned Aversive Stimuli. A stimulus which regularly precedes pain generates anxiety.

45. Conclusion: Presenting a Conditioned Aversive Stimulus results in a state of anxiety shown in part by a decrease in the food reinforced behavior and an increase in behavior which has an avoidance history.

Punishment:

46. The Conditioned Aversive Stimuli generated by regularly punish behavior will result in a state of anxiety in which positively reinforced behavior decreases and avoidance behavior increases in frequency.

47. 45. Punishment is the withdrawal of a positive reinforcer or the presentation of a negative reinforcer following a response.

Goals and Techniques of Science:

48. A respondent is always under the control of a stimulus.

49. In a reflex, response magnitude is dependent upon the intensity of the stimulus. The stimulus intensity is called the independent variable and the response magnitude the dependent variable.

50. A child who misbehaves to get attention will stop when suddenly given almost constant attention. Here the most obvious effect of getting attention is an example of satiation rather than reinforcement. If a child who has stopped misbehaving after receiving much attention is more likely to misbehave on future occasions, then "attention" reinforced misbehaving.

51. We might infer then an "anxiety neurosis" results when two incompatible responses are strong. Conditioned aversive stimuli are more or less continuously generated; hence the organism is nearly always in a state of anxiety.

Aggressiveness, Withdrawal, and Reaction Formation:

52. The aggressive person, though often reinforced, generates conditions in which others are reinforced for acting aggressively toward him. Extensive use of Aversive control results in a chronic (i.e., more or less continuous) activation syndrome with the result that the normal functioning of the body is continuously disrupted.

Notes For Chapter 4

1. A succinct summary of B.F. Skinner's theory can be found on Internet these days at the following website: Explorations into Learning and Instruction: The Theory and Practice Database. http:// tip.psychology.org/index.html.

CHAPTER 5

Sensory Stimulation

Let us begin by recapping some of the conclusions that Skinner drew from his clinical studies. In terms of Respondent Conditioning, he wrote:

> *If the presentation of a stimulus is the "cause" of a response, the two form a reflex. In a reflex, a stimulus always precedes a response.*

> *The magnitude of a stimulus is the intensity which is barely sufficient to elicit a response. In a reflex, the magnitude of the response varies with the magnitude of the stimulus. The more intense the stimulus the greater the magnitude of the response and the shorter the latency of reflex.*

And in terms of Operant Conditioning, Skinner concluded:

Reinforcement and behavior occur in temporal order. 1. Behavior 2. Reinforcement.

Food is not reinforcing unless the animal has first been deprived of food for some time.

Food is probably not reinforcing if the animal is not hungry. Unlike a stimulus in a reflex, a reinforcing stimulus does not act to elicit the response it reinforces.

When a response has been reinforced, it will be emitted more frequently in the future.

Now, in his theory of social intercourse, Berne makes the following statements:

The ability of the human psyche to maintain coherent ego states seems to depend upon a changing flow of sensory stimuli. This observation forms the psychobiological basis of social psychiatry. In structural terms, these stimuli are necessary in order to assure the integrity of the neopsyche and the archaeopsyche. If the flow is cut off or flattened into monotony, it is observed that the neopsyche gradually becomes disorganized ("The individual's thinking is impaired"); this lays bare the underlying archaeopsychic activity ("He shows childish emotional responses"); and finally archaeopsychic function becomes disorganized as well ("He suffers from hallucinations"). This is the sensory deprivation experiment.

The work of Spitz goes a little farther. It demonstrates that sensory deprivation in the infant may result not only in psychic changes, but also in organic deterioration. This shows how vital it is for the changing sensory environment to be maintained. In addition, a new and specific factor appears: the most essential and effective forms of sensory stimulation are provided by social handling and physical intimacy. Hence Spitz speaks of "emotional deprivation" rather than of "sensory deprivation". The intolerance for long periods of boredom or isolation gives rise to the concept of stimulus-hunger, particularly for the kind of stimuli offered by physical intimacy. This stimulus-hunger parallels in many ways, biologically, psychologically, and socially, the hunger for food. Such terms as malnutrition, satiation, gourmet, gourmand, faddist, ascetic, culinary arts, and good cook are easily transferred from the field of nutrition to their analogues in the field of sensation. Overstuffing has its parallel in over-stimulation, which may cause difficulties by flooding the psyche with stimuli faster than they can be comfortably handled. In both spheres, under ordinary conditions where ample supplies are available and a diversified menu is possible, choices will be heavily influenced by individual idiosyncrasies.

Fritz Perls (1969) the developer of Gestalt Therapy, states:

> . . . the great thing to understand: that awareness per-se by and of itself-can be curative. Because with full awareness you become aware of this

organismic self-regulation, you can let the organism take over without interfering, without interrupting; we can rely on the wisdom of the organism. And the contrast to this is the whole pathology of self-manipulation, environmental control, and so on, that interferes with this subtle organismic self-control (16).

I agree with Perls. If the organism is aware of what is occurring, it is capable of correcting any conflicts. However, if they have dysfunctional, or impaired sensory receptors, the organism cannot perceive the stimuli and thus is unaware of any conflict, or its resolution.

In his other book, *In and Out of the Garbage Pail,* Fritz Perls asserts that each organism has a balance point, which it is constantly striving to maintain. He compares it to maintaining a balanced budget:

> We make a habit of calling the zero point "normal." We then talk about normal temperature, normal bloodcount, etc., ad infinitum. Any plus or minus is called abnormal, a sign of malfunctioning-of illness, if the plus or minus is considerable.
>
> In the case of the biological organism, the zero point of normalcy has to be maintained or the organism will stop functioning; the organism will die.

He goes on to say: "Any disturbance of the organismic balance constitutes an incomplete gestalt, an unfinished situation forcing the organism to become creative, to find means and ways to restore that balance."

I believe that all organismic functions are dependent on the senses. Recognizing the needs of the organism and communicating those needs to the appropriate receptors, is dependent on the senses.

This brings us back to the point that Spitz makes, which Berne explained thus: *"The work of Spitz goes a little farther. It demonstrates that sensory deprivation in the infant may result not only in psychic changes, but also in organic deterioration."*

This shows how vital it is for the changing sensory environment to be maintained. In addition, a new and specific factor appears: the most essential and effective forms of sensory stimulation are provided by social handling and physical intimacy.

To repeat, as Berne stated:

> *Those idiosyncrasies which are of immediate interest to the social psychiatrist are based on archaic experiences, neopsychic judgments, and particularly in regard to physical intimacy, exteropsychic prejudices. These introduce varying amounts of caution, prudence, and deviousness into the situation, so that eventually it is only under special circumstances that the individual will make a direct gesture toward the most prized forms of stimulation represented by physical relationships. Under most conditions he will compromise. He learns to do with more subtle, even symbolic forms of handling, until the merest nod of recognition may serve the purpose to some extent, although his original craving for physical contact may remain unabated, As the complexities increase, each person becomes more and more individual in his quest, and it is these differentia which lend variety to social intercourse.*

The stimulus-hunger, with its first order sublimation into recognition-hunger, is so pervasive that the symbols of recognition become highly prized and are expected to be exchanged at every meeting between people. Deliberately withholding them constitutes a form of misbehavior called rudeness, and repeated rudeness is considered a justification for imposing social or even physical sanctions. The spontaneous forms of recognition, such as the glad smile, are most gratefully received. Other gestures, like the hiss, the obeisance, and the handshake, tend to become ritualized. In this country there is a succession of verbal gestures, each step implying more and more recognition and giving more and more gratification. This ritual may be typically summarized as follows: (a) "Hello!" (b) "How are you?" (c) "Warm enough for you?" (d) "What's new?" (e) "What else is new?" The implications are: (a) Someone is there; (b) Someone with feelings is there; (c) Someone with feelings and sensations is there; (d) Someone with feelings, sensations, and a personality is there; (e) Someone with feelings, sensations, a personality, and in whom I have more than a passing interest, is there.

A great deal of linguistic, social, and cultural structure revolves around the question of mere recognition: special pronouns, inflections, gestures, postures, gifts, and offerings are designed to exhibit recognition of status and person. The movie fan-letter is one of our indigenous products, which enables recognition to be depersonalized and quan-tified on an adding machine; and the difference

> *between the printed mimeographed, photographic,*
> *and personal reply is something like the difference*
> *between the various steps of the greeting ritual*
> *described above. The unsatisfactory nature of such*
> *mechanical recognition is shown by the preference*
> *of many actors and actresses for the live theatre over*
> *the movies, even at a considerable financial sacrifice.*
> *This is a dramatic example of the extended validity*
> *of Spitz's principle.*

The point being made is that sensory stimulation is a constant quest. Sensory stimulation is essential for the biological and psychological needs of the organism: survival is dependent upon it. This need is so great it is virtually insatiable. In observing the many youths I've worked with, it became apparent that if they didn't receive the stimuli they sought they would opt for punitive, or aversive stimuli; painful stimuli. Berne (1964) wrote:

> As far as the theory of games is concerned,
> the principle which emerges here is that any
> social intercourse whatever has a biological
> advantage over no intercourse at all. This has
> been experimentally demonstrated in the case of
> rats through some remarkable experiments by
> S. Levine, (1960), in which not only physical,
> mental and emotional development but also the
> biochemistry of the brain and even resistance to
> leukemia were favorably affected by handling. The
> significant feature of these experiments was that
> gentle handling and painful electric shocks were
> equally effective in promoting the health of the
> animals (17).

The I-2 is seen as having a bottomless pit for attention. They are often criticized for their attention getting behavior, in a derogatory manner. I believe, in the case of the I-2, because of his interpersonal relationship maturity level he has a very limited repertoire of methods for interacting with others. In as much as he functions socially as a 3- to 7-year-old child, he seeks stimulation by direct methods; he seeks to be cuddled, if that's not forthcoming he will act out to get the attention, or stimulation needed.

At the present time there is a theory being studied, Sensory Integration Dysfunction or Sensory Processing Disorder. It is believed to be caused by a neurological problem. I believe this has some merit in the case of some children. However, as for of the I-2s and I-3s I've worked with, this does not seem to be the case. They have all responded well to most stimuli, however certain stimuli, in their physical and social environment, of a low magnitude, seem to escape recognition. Where this is such a common characteristic of I-2s and I-3s, I've been lead to believe this is genetically determined. It seems the thresholds of certain receptors are too narrow to perceive certain stimuli.

This was most noted in the case of the Mp. At one point we thought the Mps were supersensitive. If an event occurred where someone was severely hurt they tended to overreact. At the same time they appeared to be insensitive to aspects of both their physical and social environments. Further observations suggested that they were unable to perceive subtle stimuli, suggesting that the thresholds of certain sensory receptors were too narrow to perceive any stimuli of a minimal magnitude.

This I believe is related to Skinner's statement:

> *The magnitude of a stimulus is the intensity which is barely sufficient to elicit a response. In a reflex, the magnitude of the response varies with the magnitude of the stimulus. The more intense the stimulus the*

greater the magnitude of the response and the shorter the latency of reflex.

In the case of the Mp, they only respond to certain stimuli appropriately, but others must be of a much greater magnitude.

As has been demonstrated by many people who have lost the sensitivity of one sense, they are able to compensate by increasing the sensitivity of other senses. As will be pointed out in the section on treatment strategies, I believe that we had inadvertently increased the sensitivity of the youths on our units.

Stimulus-Seeking Behavior

In *Sensory Deprivation: Fifteen Years of Research,* Austin Jones suggests that too much emphasis has been placed on the impairments of sensory deprivation experiments and not enough has been studied regarding the motivational value of sensory stimulation.

Subsequent studies revealed numerous theories regarding the learning process. Though each offered a rational concept, they were unable to arrive at a common conclusion including all of the theories. To do this would be like trying to find an ideal ego that could describe all people. We can only deal with generalities.

This same thing applies to suggesting that all organisms strive for a general point of maximal stimulation and that that point is common to all organisms. There are so many variables that each organism experiences, many of which are unidentifiable, that at best, we can only generalize on the sensory needs of individual organisms.

I believe that the use of generalized reinforcers actually acted as a "shotgun" type of stimulation. The generalized stimulation acted like a scatter gun; though the stimulator may intend to reinforce a specific response, the organism can conceivably apply that stimulation to wherever it feels it is needed. The organism prioritizes its activities on the basis of the greatest need. The advantage of generalized reinforcers is that they can provide stimulation for whichever sensory receptor has a need at the moment. (I believe this is illustrated in the book when describing the geriatric asking questions and the young student wanting to play instead of work; pg 89.)

Referencing Perls previously quoted statement: *"In the case of the biological organism, the zero point of normalcy has to be maintained or the organism will stop functioning; the organism will die."*

"Any disturbance of the organismic balance constitutes an incomplete gestalt, an unfinished situation forcing the organism to become creative, to find means and ways to restore that balance."

And revisiting Skinner, we will recall: *"Food is not reinforcing unless the animal has first been deprived of food for some time. Food is probably not reinforcing if the animal is not hungry."*

By using sensory stimulation as the reinforcer, for shaping human behavior, we find that its effectiveness is due to the fact that this is a near insatiable need and thus a constant quest of the human organism. In our treatment program, using sensory stimulation as a reinforcer, it seems to have been only an initial step in the process of enabling clients to successfully reach out for additional stimuli. This seems to have supported Spitz concept, as well as others, of the need for a continuous flow of stimulation.

With the various data described above and my own observations, I utilized various forms of sensory stimulation. In the process of shaping behavior, I used, as generalized reinforcers, hugs, stroking the back, recognition, compliments, encouragement, etc. In the section regarding treatment strategies, I hope to explain how this principle was applied in each case.

At this point it is hoped that the reader is beginning to see the interrelatedness of the work of Berne, Perls, Spitz, Skinner and the research of many others in developing an integrated approach to treatment of the I-2s and I-3s.

II

Basic Treatment Strategy

CHAPTER I

Basic Treatment Program

In 1964, a program was developed in the Pioneer Lodge of the California Youth Authority's Fricot School for Boys, for youths eight to twelve years old. These children were considered among the most difficult to deal with. At the time, the CYA's Reasearch Division reported that 10% of our wards had a 90% recidivism rate in a six-month period. It was stated that this group simply didn't fit our programs but had been assigned to the CYA because they were intolerable in the community and there were no other programs available. The introduction of specific techniques and concepts, that didn't include medication, resulted in a 17% recidivism rate in a 2 1/2 year period.

Based on my prior experiences at the CYA's Preston School of Industry, I recognized the fact that of any group of people there are leaders, followers and scapegoats. I also noted that, of those experiencing a therapeutic environment, some were successful on parole while others failed and were soon returned. Having seen dramatic changes in some of our wards and not others, I attempted to identify the things that those who succeeded did that the failures didn't do.

The Pioneer Lodge was a twenty-boy unit whose purpose was to house the most difficult of the younger youths committed to the CYA, (ages seven to twelve). It was named after Fritz Redl's "Pioneer Lodge." The initial treatment plan followed the model described in the book he co-authored, *The Aggressive Child*. As he had had limited results with only minimal lasting effects, so had the initial program at the CYA's Pioneer Lodge. Other methods followed with about the same results (this is an assumption of mine based on the reports of my staff, who were either a part of those programs or were aware of the activities of the unit).

When I took charge of the unit, as Senior Group Supervisor, it was with the understanding that our goal was to develop a new and innovative treatment program. My previous assignment began with difficult youths of an older age range. That unit became an experimental group in the CYA's search for effective treatment plans. With the knowledge gained from that program, I was able to formulate an experimental treatment model. The plan seemed feasible to both the administration and to my staff; it was new and different. Here are our notes from our first team meeting:

Notes From the First Team Meeting of the Pioneer Staff

1. To develop a program which would serve the best of Fricot traditions, support the "Block System" ("Treatment Team Approach"), maintain its "Home Life Unit" identity and yet be so unique as to justify the existence of Pioneer Lodge under its present status; a twenty-boy unit with staffing equal to that of the larger units of 50-60 youths.

2. Plans: Immediate, Short range and Long range for achieving goals of the unit.

A. Long Range

Though no conclusions were drawn during our initial planning, there were feelings expressed that achieving our goals could feasibly benefit not only Pioneer Lodge and Fricot, but possibly the whole CYA.

B. Short Range

Establishment of three sub-groups structured and programmed in such a manner so as to meet individual needs and in turn supporting the overall living unit program and a community living concept.

C. Immediate Plans

Selection of youths to form the sub-groups.

I began with the premise that all groups of people are divided into three sub-groups: leaders, followers and scapegoats. The individual's position in the hierarchy had some undefinable yet major influence on his success or failure as a parolee. I proposed a plan whereby our unit would be divided into three groups, placing the leaders in one, the followers in another and the scapegoats into still another. In my prior experience at the CYA Preston School, we had, on an experimental basis, progressively added new experimental treatment programs to our existing programs.

The success was such that I suggested that the treatment techniques we might employ would be individual counseling, small group counseling, community meetings, recreational activities that were comprised of one, two, or all three groups, academic class work, and housecleaning chores. To achieve this plan, we devised an elaborate time schedule that enabled all of our wards to have equal opportunities to experience beneficial social interaction, which we assumed they could learn.

At the initial presentation of my plan, Cal Terhune, the Assistant Superintendent and administrative overseer of the program, stated that my proposal very closely paralleled that of the CYA's "Community Treatment Project" (CTP), being conducted in the Stockton parole division. He suggested that we investigate their program and arranged for a meeting with their staff.

The meeting with the CTP staff proved to be very productive. We were introduced to the I-Level Theory. This theory is described in detail in the 1957 article, "The Development of Interpersonal Maturity: Applications to Delinquency," which appeared in *Psychiatry:*

> This typology is an elaboration of the Sullivan,
> Grant and Grant Levels of Interpersonal
> Maturity, a theoretical formulation describing a
> sequence of personality integrations in normal
> childhood development. This classification system
> focuses upon the ways in which the child is able
> to see himself and the world, especially in terms
> of emotions and motivations; i.e., his ability to
> understand what is happening between himself
> and others as well as between others. (373-385)

The I-Level typology provided an accurately detailed description of those youths I had only described in generalized terms. With the data provided by the CTP, the division of our unit was determined by the youths' I-Level: 2s, 3s and 4s. After several months of observing our group in both homogeneous and heterogeneous activities, and in as much as I had originally intended to design a program for that 10% of our wards for whom their was no program, we decided to focus on the I-2s. Our decision was based on a conclusion that we had achieved almost unbelievable results in a relatively short period of time.

In a homogeneous setting, the I-2s were far more manageable and were more responsive to meaningful learning experiences. I-2s, characteristically, have a very low tolerance for stress. Observing the marked improvement in their tolerance when in a homogeneous setting, we assumed that the presence of other personality types was stressful to I-2s. We also found that their behavioral changes were having a lasting affect.

The program developed succeeded by maintaining specific principles:

1. Providing for meaningful learning experiences
2. A rigid and consistent time structuring
3. Recognition that all wards had problems. That's why they were there. Cooperatively helping each other overcome their particular problem.
4. Perseverance
5. Recognition of progressive regressions as part of the learning process
6. Encouragement and recognition of all effort
7. Open communications between staff members regarding wards
8. Freedom to err: minimal dependence on staff to control behavior
9. Sensory stimulation
10. Staff attitude
11. Sophisticated Operant Conditioning
    a. Stress free environment
    b. Behavioral goals-moral values
    c. Stimuli-Recognition

Perfection cannot be improved upon. The best science can do is explain fragments of human behavior, and then only speculatively.

Man cannot conceive all of the interrelated aspects of human behavior to all universal factors; he can't even identify all these factors. This is not to say that legitimate scientific evidence is wrong, but the use of that evidence constructively is speculative and based on man's values, which are not always in harmony with unidentified universal laws. How often have these speculations been proven wrong over time?

A short while ago, Steve Allen wrote a book claiming that our society had lowered its standards and opted for mediocrity. The truth of the matter is, I believe, that we have raised our standards and have made the false assumption that anyone can learn anything, and to a common degree of proficiency. The facts are that not all people have the same talents and there are many things that many people cannot achieve to any degree of proficiency. Consequently, as our standards have risen, the number of talented people capable of achieving those standards have diminished. Mediocrity is a value judgment when compared to expectations of perfection. When compared to the skills of the individual, individual achievement can well be perfection within the range of their given talents.

Society, in almost every area of human endeavor, is repeating the same sins of the Pharisees—setting standards that can't be met.

In the introduction to the I-Level Theory, the "Theoretical Frame of Reference" states:

> *Each of the seven stages or levels is defined by a crucial interpersonal problem, which must be a solved before further progress toward maturity can occur. All persons do not necessarily work their way through each stage but may become fixed at a particular level.*

This may be true of I-4s and higher maturity levels, but I don't believe this is true of I-2s and I-3s.

In Berne's book, *Games People Play,* Perls is quoted as saying, "The attainment of autonomy is manifested by the release or recovery of three capacities; awareness, spontaneity and intimacy."

(p.178) In the case of the I-2s and I-3s their awareness is limited by the functionality of certain sensory receptors. If the incoming sensory stimuli don't fall within the thresholds of the receptors or the receptors are simply dysfunctional, no awareness occurs, and thus there is no response from the organism.

I believe the I-levels described in the I-level theory actually represent their maximum potential. When things are going their way, many can function quite well. When things are not going their way, this is when the symptoms described become apparent. The cause and effect vary with each I-level, but the cause and effect are basically the same within each type. This is the basis for the need of differential treatment. Because of the idiosyncrasies of each of the I-2 and I-3 types, they cannot respond to traditional treatment methods, nor can they be expected to achieve higher maturity levels. Given treatment appropriate to their personality type, they can learn to simply function better in their physical and social environment.

Initially, I attempted to develop a universal treatment plan for all delinquent youths; however, with the introduction of the I-Level Theory and their goal of differential treatment, I looked for the specific needs of each of the I-Level types. I later came to realize that the universal treatment plan that I had devised was actually beneficial to each of the types. Each type was able to benefit according to his individual needs. The treatment plan was eventually refined to ten specific objectives, which the wards were expected to make an effort to do. These 10 points were as follows:

1. Helping others
2. Individual counseling
3. Small group counseling
4. Large group meeting

5. Indoor activities
6. Outdoor activities
7. School
8. Living unit cleanup
9. Peer relationships
10. Staff relationships

At the time, my intent was to provide as many opportunities as I could for the wards to learn social skills in various situations. This was based on the assumption that given enough meaningful learning experiences they could progress to the next I-level as suggested in the I-level report. However, on the basis of further studies and experience, I concluded that they weren't able to progress to the next I-level but were able to function better, improve their interpersonal relationship skills, increase their sensitivity to their physical and social environment, and reduce their aggressiveness.

The following graph indicates the growth process. In Skinner's clinical studies he found that learning specific tasks could be illustrated by a single line of continuous progressions. Educators have indicated that learning is best illustrated with a curve. My observations led me to believe that our youths seemed to go through learning cycles. By tracking the behavior and involvement in the program of a random group of youths, using three observers, I was able to graphically illustrate this phenomenon. Though our youths were of the same personality types, they seemed to have different intellects, came from different socio-economic backgrounds and from different geographical locations.

Yet, in spite of these differences, they all went through the same periodic cycles. With this awareness, I was able to predict, with some degree of accuracy, what phase of their cycle they were in and then be able to encourage and support them through their regression.

Behavior

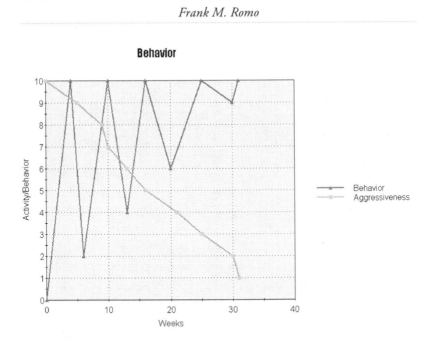

Activity/Behavior = Involvement in the 10 point objectives

At one point, it was suggested that they were going through the cycles due to suggestion on my part. Initially, I said nothing to the wards about these learning cycles. I watched them to see how they were handling the regressions. It was a struggle for them to proceed to the next cycle. These were youths whose lives were filled with failures.

To see if I could break these cycles, I began by explaining the cycles to the wards and then encouraging them to keep working on the 10 points. I explained that the more they worked on the 10 points, the sooner they would overcome the regression. Though my explanation had little effect on changing the cycles, it did ease the stress they were experiencing. Instead of seeing themselves as failures (they all had low self-esteems), they were able to understand that their regressions were actually part of their progress.

I chose to call the regressions "progressive regressions." As can be noted on the chart, each regression was less than the previous one. The initial regression was the most severe. On the surface, it appeared that no progress had been made. However, on closer observation, it could be seen that some progress had been made. Of course, as each of the ensuing regressions occurred, it became more obvious that progress was being made.

I believe that the regressions were a necessary part of the progressions. In as much as the human organism is an integrated whole, when something affective occurs to one part of the organism, other parts are also affected. I believe the regressions are periods in which the other parts are adapting to the changes.

After six to eight months in the program, the disparity between the progressions and regressions was minimal. The progressions and regressions became merely responses to the natural courses of events in daily living. As each of us have new experiences in our daily lives, we experience ups and downs, adaptations to the new experiences.

I believe Skinner's explanation of the speed with which a pigeon acquired a key pecking response also explains the progression/regression phenomenon:

> *Pigeon C's record does not reveal the speed of acquiring a key pecking response because other processes are also involved. The pigeon must first adapt to the box and the click. Conditioning can occur very fast when adaptation is already complete and when each response is immediately reinforced.*

When a youth first arrives on the unit, he is met by the unit social worker who interviews him, makes an initial evaluation, assigns him to a particular caseworker and briefly explains the treatment program to him.

Once assigned to a caseload, he is interviewed by his caseworker, who in turn makes an evaluation and begins building a relationship with the youth, explaining more about the living unit and answering any questions the youth may have. As his day progresses, he is usually welcomed by others on the same caseload, who also reassure him and explain the unit's daily procedures. He will also experience the daily community meeting. Both peers and staff make an effort to reassure him and alleviate any fantasized fears he might have.

Modified Therapeutic Community

To some, this may be a difficult concept to comprehend. Explaining it is difficult. I'll do my best to define and clarify its principles.

In a therapeutic community the inmates established their own values, by consensus, through their Community Meetings. In as much as they are creating their own rules to live by, each is held accountable by the community.

Most institutional settings have a list of rules that all must conform to. Often, the participants are either given a printed copy of the rules or the rules are posted in a conspicuous place. In contrast, the therapeutic community has no pre-established rules per se, but is intended to assimilate conditions found in the community, outside the institution. We hope to teach them those things pertinent to the interpersonal relationships between the individual and the community.

To achieve this, the boys are given as many opportunities of self determined behavior as possible, within the permissible limits of established security procedures. It is hoped that the increased opportunities to succeed or fail would accelerate the opportunities for meaningful learning experiences. (This seemingly permissive environment also allows for a variety of stimuli. See chapter on Sensory Stimulation).

Though the program assumes an air of permissiveness, such is not the intent. Behavior tolerances remain as close as possible to those found in the general populace.

No Rules

One of the first questions asked by most Mps is, "What are the rules?"

This question came up at one of our community meetings. One of the wards gave one of the best explanations and one that they all understood. He said, "We don't have rules, we have procedures, though." The point he was making was that we didn't have behavioral rules per se; but to facilitate such things as wake-up time, mealtimes, school time, meeting times, etc., we had to follow some sort of regime, thus, procedures.

The chart below shows the "procedures" he was referring to, this rigid time structure we had in place:

Time Structure

Day/Time	Monday	Tuesday	Wednesday	Thursday	Friday	Saturday	Sunday
6:00-7:00	!	Wash-up	And	Breakfast	!	Wash &	Breakfast
7:00-8:00	←	Clean-up	Prepare	for	School	C↑	
8:00-9:00	↑	T: SG					
9:00-10:00	S L: SW	T: SW	P.E,			L ↑	Church↑
10:00-11:00	C P.E.					E V	L:SG V
11:00-12:00	H N: SG					A↓I	I
12:00-1:00	O ←			Lunch		N S	→ S
1:00-2:00	O					T: SG I	I
2:00-3:00	L R: SG	P.E./R:SW	C: SW	R: SG	P.E./H: SW	L:FC T	T
3:00-4:00	↓ ←	Community		Meetings	→	H:FC↓	→
4:00-5:00	H: SG	L: SG	C: SG	N: SG	H: SG		R:FC
5:00-6:00	↑		Dinner			U	↑
6:00-7:00	↑		Recreation			P	↑
7:00-8:00	↑		Recreation				↑
8:00-9:00	↑		Showers	&	Cleanup		↑
9:00-10:00	↑			Bedtime			
Key to Chart:	SG = Small Group	SW = Social Worker	FC = Family Counseling	Caseworkers by initial: T,R,H,N, & L			

In other words:

School: 9:00-3:00 Monday to Friday
Community Meetings: 3:00-4:00 Monday to Friday
Clean-up: 8:00-12:00 Saturdays, 7:00-8:00 AM and 8:00-9:00 PM daily
Two small group meetings per week
Recreation: 6:00-9:00 PM and during periods when some are in Small Group meetings
Visiting and Family Counseling: on weekends, 10:00 AM - 5:00 PM

This time structure served many purposes:

1. I was striving to create a clinic-like environment with consistency and minimal variables.
2. I-2s and I-3s are means-oriented as opposed to goal oriented. Both have limited insight and foresight which limits their ability to predict the behavior of others and to understand what is expected of them. Consistent structuring relieves stress and improves their ability to function.
3. It also assured us that each ward had an equal opportunity to achieve his treatment goals.
4. It encouraged the wards to assume more responsibility for their actions. Staff was discouraged from reminding them of their responsibilities. The wards assumed responsibility to encourage others to meet their responsibilities. This helped increase their awareness of others.
5. As each time period arrived, the wards were ready for the activity. We hoped to develop their foresight and responsibility.

In assimilating the atmosphere of the outside community, it was recognized that there are no lists of rules out there; yet all the wards knew the general mores of their community. By giving them the opportunity to make poor choices, it provided us an opportunity to teach them appropriate options. We felt that if they didn't learn these things in the institution, they wouldn't learn them in the community.

Case Conferences

During a ward's first month, he meets with the total staff in what is called a "Case Conference." During his initial conference, he establishes his treatment goals. He is asked what he would like to change about himself while he is on the unit. Though he has undoubtedly been told by his peers what to expect and what is acceptable, amazingly, the ward shows insight in selecting realistic goals and suggesting what the staff might do to help them achieve these goals. Every two months following his initial case conference, he has additional case conferences to evaluate his progress. At these times, he discusses with staff his progress, his strengths and weaknesses, and areas in which he might need to extend his effort.

The purpose of case conferences is to encourage and support the efforts of the youth to achieve his goals. It is not intended to be used as an aversive stimulus to intimidate or coerce the youth. It is intended to demonstrate a genuine concern of the staff for the youth's welfare.

The last three paragraphs illustrate 1, 9 and 10 of the program objectives to help them achieve their treatment goals. Their peers were helping them with their reassurance. They were also demonstrating appropriate peer relations. The staff, in their interviews, were building ward/staff relationships. In contrast to the meeting that I described in the introduction, the staff and wards were genuinely concerned about each other. This theme was encouraged in each of their activities. Narcissism and destructive criticism were tabooed.

In fact, the wards developed a motto, by referring to a comment by Flower, of the Disney movie *Bambi,* in which Flower quoted his mother: "If you can't say something nice to a person, don't say nothing." This of course was supported in their meetings where "strokes" were explained, taught and encouraged.

Occasionally, through attrition, with new wards, I would reiterate a statement that seemed effective in deterring destructive peer relations and encourage cooperative concern. I would point out that everyone there had a problem; if he didn't, he wouldn't be there. Being confined was not the most desirable way to live. The way they related to one another could make it worse. However, if they worked together to help each other, life could be more tolerable and could help shorten their stay. This, of course, was supported and encouraged by the 10 point objectives. Their efforts in each of these 10 areas as well as their progress toward their treatment goals were evaluated at the Case Conference interview.

Relationship Building

Treatment begins with the relationship between the client and the therapist (teacher, parent, caregiver, grandparent, employer, doctor, etc.). The initial contact sets the stage for relationship development. People are often surprised when they find they've misjudged someone's personality. Their surprise is indicative of the fact that this is a rare occasion. We communicate who and what we are primarily by non-verbal cues.

Researchers determined that just 7% of what we communicate is the result of the words that we say or the content of our communication. Thirty-eight percent of our communication to others is a result of our verbal behavior, which includes tone of voice, timbre, cadence, inflection, tempo and volume. Fifty-five percent of our communication to others is a result of our non-verbal communication—our facial expressions, body posture, breathing, skin color changes and our movements. The match between our verbal and non-verbal communication indicates the level of congruency. Mastery of non-verbal communication is essential for the mastery of interpersonal relationships.

As we proceed through treatment strategies, I will point out how significant this is for the practitioner to successfully treat each of the specific personalities described. Diagnosis of the client's personality influences the approach to use in the relationship building process.

Many people who care for others have innate skills that enable them to establish relationships quite rapidly. They are usually people who sincerely care for their clients, have a warm smile, a sense of humor, sensitivity to the needs of their clients, empathetic, enthusiastic, encouraging, patient, clinically consistent and persevering. They can be great practitioners. Given adequate knowledge, they can better help their clients achieve whatever their goals may be.

I have worked with many with these talents. Though they were talented, they seemed unable to achieve the same results as I did, using what appeared to be the same methods. My results were so consistent, given the time and opportunity, I realized I must have been using some very subtle techniques that were difficult to accurately identify. Many times co-workers attempted to identify those subtleties without certain success.

In the process of writing this book I've done much self-analysis and analysis of others who seemed to have the potential for the same success. My description above seems to describe the characteristics needed. However, if the methods described in this Treatment Strategies section are adhered to, I believe this can improve anyone's success rate. The difference between consistent and inconsistent results is dependent on consistency. There is little room for prejudice or inconsistency. If the methods work, use them. If they don't, change them. In most cases of failure, it's the agent that must change.

Counseling

1) Individual Counseling

Individual counseling covered points 2 and 10 of their 10 point objectives. Many of our youths were apprehensive about talking to authoritative figures and even more apprehensive of discussing their feelings. Where the youths were expected to arrange a meeting with their caseworker at least once a week, this helped them counter their apprehension. No specific topic was expected to be discussed. Sometimes the ward chose the subject and sometimes the caseworker made the choice. One of the purposes of the meeting was to discuss his progress, but more importantly, it was to help him learn how to relate and build a relationship.

One youth that I had on my caseload arrived with a "bad mouth." Most people would describe him as a "wise-mouthed punk." However, in observing my relationships with other wards and particularly within our small group, he began to settle down. In one of our small group meetings, in response to a conversation between some others in the group, he asked, "Weren't you afraid?" I don't recall what he was referring to, but a few days later in our meeting, I gently asked him what his fear was about. He related to me that when he was in the third grade, reciting before the class, the teacher ridiculed him, intensifying his fear and embarrassing him beyond his ability to cope. He ran out of the classroom and never returned to school. He also related to me that he was afraid of everything, especially people.

This was a sixteen-year-old Mp who was moving toward an intimate relationship. This relationship developed to the point that he became a youth that was a pleasure to be around. In the classroom, the wards were started at their tested academic level and then allowed progress at their own speed. This youth began at the third grade level. In the eight months he was in the program, he progressed to the grade level appropriate to his chronological age.

This was not an isolated case, but an occasion that we experienced many times over. This only represented two points of the 10 point program, but the 10 points complemented each other in such a way that they work together collectively to bring about the desired results.

2) Small Group Counseling

When we first began small group counseling, it was still in its infancy and experimental stage. At Preston, we began with some of the methods employed by the Chinese Communists in their brainwashing during the Korean War. The staff, at that time, were all layman with high school degrees and some with some college experience. Six units were chosen to experiment with the small group concept. We began by trying reflective counseling. We then moved on to role reversal counseling.

Next, we tried directed counseling. After several weeks, I was told that most of the other units had given up small group counseling. I was asked why I continued. My response was that I couldn't identify what was happening, but I sensed something positive was happening, so I continued.

I had three groups during this period. Each group was begun fresh and continued until attrition reduced the number in the group. Each meeting was recorded. In reviewing my records, I discovered that all three groups went through specific phases before they finally became a cohesive and productive group.

At Fricot, because we were dealing with younger youths and primarily I-2s, we decided to have activity-oriented groups coupled with "guided growth."

At O.H. Close, we proceeded to use the same method we used at Preston: directed counseling and forming new groups as attrition determined. Shortly after our beginning at O.H. Close, the social worker informed me that the treatment of some wards was delayed while waiting for a new group to begin. He suggested that we have ongoing groups. I had no idea what the effects would be, but I agreed to give it a try. We found that ongoing groups were far more productive than new groups, determined by attrition. It gave new members an opportunity to adapt and to learn from other wards the benefits of participation.

Shortly after the opening of O.H. Close, we were introduced to and given extensive training in Transactional Analysis (TA). We were also introduced to Gestalt Therapy and the work of Fritz Perls. This made small group counseling far more productive and gave **far more meaning** to the overall program.

I-2s and I-3s have limited insight and foresight; therefore, they are not amenable to traditional insight therapy. I-3s, however, with TA therapy coupled with the overall program were able to increase their insight and their awareness of their social and physical environment.

Using TA, the wards were educated in the concepts of TA and social interaction. Each ward was also given an opportunity to discuss these concepts and their relationship to his own behavior. Occasionally, a meeting would seem slow to begin, so a member would be asked what he wanted to work on in that meeting. It was rare for a youth to decline. Most youths anticipated the small group meetings and were prepared to discuss their "hang-ups." They also knew that this was one of the 10 points that they were expected to participate in.

The rules of the small groups were few, but they were expected to remain seated, to refrain from any destructive criticisms and not to discuss, outside of the group, anything discussed during the meeting.

The following is a list of subjects discussed and analyzed during our small group meetings:

1. Regressive analysis to identify behavior patterns for analysis
2. Sensory stimulation
3. Nonverbal communication
4. Strokes, giving and receiving
5. Dream analysis (Perl's method)
6. Family relationships
7. Peer relationships
8. Sibling relationships
9. Home community activities and relationships
10. School involvement
11. Commitment crimes
12. Sexual relationships
13. The 10-point program and their involvement
14. Analysis of their behavior, on the unit, by other members of the group (positive criticism and suggestions)
15. In one case I used a ward, an I-4, as a co-therapist. He had been on the unit for a long term and had made unusual progress.
16. Relationship building
17. Behavioral chains and blocking the chains
18. Identification of and analysis of feelings
19. Alternative behaviors, choices
20. Education: Explaining the significance and interrelatedness of many aspects of daily living.
21. Actually, any subject they wanted to discuss and its relationship to their behavior.

Community Meetings

Community meetings were primarily designed to discuss and work through any subjects that affected communal living. Any conclusions drawn in the meetings, by consensus, were to be adhered to by all members of the community. Everyone is accountable to the community and all are expected to hold each other accountable.

At O.H. Close, we utilized a modified therapeutic community whereby the administrators still had to approve the desires of the community. Community meetings served many purposes besides the functioning of the community. There are many subtle dynamics that occur during the meetings.

Subtle benefits of community meetings beside community functions:

1. Speaking to a large group
2. Listening to others in a large group
3. Speaking and listening to others with respect
4. Recognizing and appreciating views other than their own
5. Submitting to the will of others without a loss of identity
6. Insightful discussion without narcissism, cynicism or skepticism
7. Compromise and cooperation
8. Raising self-esteem
9. Encouraging and supporting others
10. Increased understanding of peers and staff
11. Increased awareness of value of self and others
12. Recognizing and appreciating the value of others without prejudices
13. Loyalty and pride in their community; community identity
14. Responsibility
15. Respect for their physical environment
16. Respect for the property of others and their right to ownership

This is not a complete list, and these benefits didn't apply to all wards; but those that needed these benefits acquired them in part from the community meetings.

Whenever a ward had an objection, or suggestion, that might benefit others, he was encouraged to bring it up at the meeting for discussion.

Critiques of the meetings, by the staff, kept all aware of what was occurring in all areas of the wards and staff activities. This was beneficial in supporting the endeavors of each staff member and the efforts of both the community and individual wards. It also kept communications open between the staff members.

In the case of Mps, this is essential. Areas in which the Mp is unable to perceive the realities of what has occurred, he will fabricate the series of events that have led up to his misbehavior. He then either denies his behavior, or projects the blame to another or to circumstances. This is a form of lying. On the other hand, true liars know what the truth is; however, in most situations, the Mp doesn't know what has really occurred. In keeping communications open between staff members, the truth can be exposed and dealt with. This is the foundation for the "treatment team" approach.

Some other units, using a reasonable facsimile of the program described, based their evaluation of community meetings on the original concept, "functioning of the unit." Several reduced the number of meetings they had to one to three meetings a week. I insisted on continuing the daily meetings because I saw the influence the meetings had on wards. Their prestige and self-esteem could be observed progressing from initial passivity to active participation. This was most noticeable among the Cfms. There was much more occurring than simply improving the community's functioning. As previously stated, my goal was to help delinquents become non-delinquents and to help dysfunctional youths become more successfully functional.

Community meetings proved to be one more integral tool complementing the basic treatment plan and its purpose.

Chapter 2

Punishment

Though punishment was not a particular subject that we dwelt on nor felt significant enough in our treatment model to thoroughly explore, I felt it was necessary to include this subject in my book because I was questioned several times as to how we were able to maintain control without some form of punishment.

As our program developed, the attitude of the staff changed as well as that of the wards in our charge. In the early stages, various periods of isolation were used and were dependent on the particular infraction. In the latter stages, the relationship between wards and staff had changed dramatically. With rare exception, the worst infraction was an occasional fight. The matter was quickly resolved as soon as the wards calmed down enough to discuss their difficulty. Occasionally the matter was referred to the Community Meeting. At other times it was discussed at his case conference. If a ward was unable to regain his composure, he was referred to the isolation ward until he calmed down and was able to discuss the problem.

Punishment is a relatively complex subject which is misused too frequently. What is generally considered common knowledge is based on erroneous assumptions. Too often the misuse of punishment can, in many cases, reinforce the very behavior that the punisher is striving to extinguish.

I've chosen to elaborate on the subject to benefit caregivers, that they may be more efficient and more successful in shaping behavior. The initial notes may be difficult for the caregiver to understand or perceive their relatedness. However, knowing this data is necessary to understand the examples and illustrations that follow, which, in turn can help the reader understand:

Punishment is the withdrawal of a positive reinforcer or the presentation of a negative reinforcer following a response.

Reinforcement which consists of presenting stimuli (e.g. food) is called positive reinforcement.

In contrast, reinforcement which consists of terminating stimuli (e.g. painful stimuli) is called negative reinforcement.

Stimuli accompanying or just preceding a punished response become Conditioned Aversive Stimuli by being paired with the punisher.

Because the response does not appear to be produced by an eliciting stimulus, it is said to be emitted. The Conditioned Aversive Stimulus is an eliciting stimulus.

The punisher may be anything that elicits the activation syndrome.

For example: A child misbehaves. He is punished following the misbehavior. The punishment becomes a conditioned aversive stimuli by being paired with the punisher.

The Conditioned Aversive Stimuli generated by regularly punished behavior will result in a state of anxiety in which positively reinforced behavior decreases and avoidance behavior increases in frequency.

Regardless of the effectiveness of punishment, an Aversive Stimulus used as a punisher will elicit the respondents (sweating, increased heart rate, etc.) comprising the activation syndrome, which occurs in many emotional states. A single Aversive Stimulus used in punishment elicits respondents, conditions other stimuli to elicit the respondents, and makes possible the conditioning of avoidance behavior. The single Aversive Stimulus has multiple effects. Two ways of effectively preventing unwanted conditioned behavior are
(1) to extinguish it by withholding reinforcement and (2) to condition some incompatible behavior.

Shaping Behavior

There are two aspects in shaping skillful behavior: reinforcing only certain responses, which is called (1) differential reinforcement, and gradually raising the requirement for reinforcement, which is called (2) successive approximations.

Responses reinforced by the generalized reinforcers of affection, approval, etc., often are extinguished very slowly because the subtlety of the stimuli has made the schedule intermittent.

It is more than simple conditioning when we differentially reinforce successive approximations to a final form of behavior. When we follow the procedure, we are said to be "shaping behavior." For best results in shaping behavior, the Conditioned reinforcer should be presented in a close temporal relation to the response.

Behavior must be not only acquired but also maintained in strength by reinforcement. Under continuous reinforcement, after reaching a maximum rate, an Operant is maintained in maximal strength only if it continues to be reinforced. In the early Conditioning of a response, reinforcement must be rather frequent (preferably continuous); if this is not the case, the response may be extinguished before the next reinforcement is due.

You may show affection or approval to reinforce the response you want another person to
emit more frequently. You may withhold affection or approval to extinguish behavior you don't want another person to emit.

Avoidance and Escape Behavior

Before a positive reinforcer, such as food, can be used effectively, we must arrange an appropriate state of deprivation. Similarly, before termination of a shock can reinforce a response, we must first present a shock. A stimulus which reinforces behavior which terminates it, is called a negative reinforcer, or an Aversive Stimulus.

In avoidance behavior, a response is emitted before the Aversive Stimulus occurs and the response delays or prevents the stimulus. The reinforcement for an avoidance response is the termination of a Conditioned Aversive Stimulus. In successful avoidance, the unconditioned Aversive Stimulus is not presented.

A dog might jump from a compartment before a shock is delivered in the case of avoidance behavior or might jump after the shock is delivered in the case of escape behavior.

In avoidance behavior the subject anticipates the aversive stimulus.

In escape behavior the subject responds after the aversive stimulus is presented.

When a child knows he will be punished for a specific behavior, by not doing that behavior he avoids the punishment. If, while being punished for misbehavior, he runs away, this is escape behavior. In shaping behavior, we must first determine the desired behavior. What is the behavior you want the child to emit, or what is the behavior you want a child to avoid?

Do we want a child to learn specific behaviors, or specific tasks?

Do we want them to avoid painful experiences?

If we want a child to avoid touching a hot stove, we use aversive (painful) stimuli each time he reaches for the stove.

If we want him to learn his alphabet, we use positive reinforcement for each effort.

Remember Berne's theory of social contact?

> *The ability of the human psyche to maintain coherent ego states seems to depend upon a changing flow of sensory stimuli. This observation forms the psychobiological basis of social psychiatry. In structural terms, these stimuli are necessary in order to assure the integrity of the neopsyche and the archaeopsyche. If the flow is cut off or flattened into monotony, it is observed that the neopsyche gradually becomes disorganized ("The individual's thinking is impaired"); this lays bare the underlying archaeopsychic activity ("He shows childish emotional responses"); and finally, archaeopsychic function becomes disorganized as well ("He suffers from hallucinations"). This is the sensory deprivation experiment.*

and as previously quoted from the same author:

> *The work of Spitz goes a little farther. It*
> *demonstrates that sensory deprivation in the infant*
> *may result not only in psychic changes, but also in*
> *organic deterioration. This shows how vital it is for*
> *the changing sensory environment to be maintained.*
> *In addition, a new and specific factor appears:*
> *the most essential and effective forms of sensory*
> *stimulation are provided by social handling and*
> *physical intimacy. Hence Spitz speaks of "emotional*
> *deprivation" rather than of "sensory deprivation".*
> *The intolerance for long periods of boredom or*
> *isolation gives rise to the concept of stimulus-hunger,*
> *particularly for the kind of stimuli offered by*
> *physical intimacy. This stimulus-hunger parallels in*
> *many ways, biologically, psychologically, and socially,*
> *the hunger for food. Such terms as malnutrition,*
> *satiation, gourmet, gourmand, faddist, ascetic,*
> *culinary arts, and good cook are easily transferred*
> *from the field of nutrition to their analogues in the*
> *field of sensation.*

The results of sensory deprivation experiments plus the work of Spitz implies that sensory stimulation is a primary need of the organism if the psyche is to maintain its integrity. In my work I reasoned that if sensory stimulation is paired with generalized reinforcers, they could become ideal reinforcers. They are always immediately available, there is always a need (the need for sensory stimulation is near insatiable). In shaping the behavior of subjects, by continuous reinforcement with physical strokes, such as hugs, pats on the back, etc., initially, and at the same time pairing them with the generalized reinforcers of affection and approval, the general reinforcers become as effective as the physical strokes. As these reinforcers prove to be effective, I change the reinforcement schedule to an intermittent one. Soon the generalize reinforcers become as effective as the touch. Because this is paired with the task as well, the task itself becomes a reinforcer.

Thus we find that punishment can provide an effective method for shaping behavior to avoid painful stimuli. We also find that shaping behavior by reinforcing successive approximations is effective in achieving a desired behavior. Children raised in a critical and punitive environment frequently experience the conditioned aversive stimuli, which results in a state of anxiety in which positively reinforced behavior decreases and avoidance behavior increases in frequency. This can ultimately debilitate the child due to a continual state of anxiety. Adhering to the prescribed methods of shaping behavior will enhance a person's ability to function at an optimal level of performance.

Now that we have outlined the basic treatment plan, we must take a look at how the plan can accommodate individual strategies per type. The following section borrows largely from the by now familiar report, *Interpersonal Maturity Level Classification: Juvenile Diagnosis and Treatment of Low, Middle and High Maturity Delinquents*, in order to detail the background characteristics inherent to each type. I then look at the treatment strategies for each and offer my own conclusions based on my observations and experiences.

III

Individual Treatment Strategies

CHAPTER I

The I-2

Characteristics of the I-2 Population (Low Maturity):

1. Approximate equivalents in other classification systems; Disorganized Personality, Maladaptive Delinquent (Jenkins), Unsocialized Aggressive Delinquent, Receiver (Studt), Aggressive Delinquent—Type E(Gibbons-Garrity),Schizophrenic, possible brain damage of unknown origin, ADDH, Hyperactive

Ways of Perceiving the World:

2. <u>Sees the world as giver or withholder</u>. His relationships with others are centered on whether they give him or deny him. The world should take care of him, but ordinarily doesn't do an adequate job. He does not perceive himself as needing to contribute anything.

3. <u>Thoroughly egocentric</u> - no cathexes for non-self. Does not get emotionally involved with objects or people beyond his own needs. Life's experiences are described

in terms of his own needs, his responses, his wants, his frustrations, and his self-concerns.

4. <u>Undifferentiated view of others</u>. Since nothing exists for him except his own way of looking at things, he sees the actions of others as arbitrary and unmotivated by feelings, each act independent of any organized personality system. Since he has no awareness of feelings in others, he is unable to understand what others are doing to him or what they expect of him. He shows little agreement with others about reality.

5. <u>People as barriers to his satisfactions</u>. Sees the arbitrary and unpredictable actions of others as the principal cause of his frustrations. Constant perception of others as denying him, with no understanding of reasons.

6. <u>Unrealistic optimism re future</u>. In spite of the difficulties and conflicts, which he describes in his past, he faces the future with high hopes and no realistic plans. He anticipates very little personal trouble in the future once he is free of authoritative restrictions (including Agent and agency). Extreme discrepancy between actual achievement level and his felt capacity to achieve.

7. <u>High incidence of magical distortion</u>. Exaggerated belief in his own powers and abilities and exaggerated belief in his own importance to others. May even believe he is predestined for greatness. Failure may intensify or rigidify this pattern or may lead to orgies of self-pity.

8. <u>A "receiver" of life's impact</u>. Feels the victim of life with no controls over self and future. He does not choose goals and strive toward them; unfortunate things just happen to him. He feels the victim of an unreasonable, inexorable, hostile and confusing world. Feels buffeted

about by passing events, perceiving stress where none would exist for the normal personality.

9. <u>Not a "generator."</u> Does not perceive himself as a contributor to response in others. Does not perceive the connection between his feelings and behavior and the response of others to him.

Ways of Responding to the World:

10. <u>Resentment of denying figures.</u> Someone or something must be to blame for his lack of need fulfillment. May constantly complain about some past adult figures or agencies for not taking care of him properly or not giving him what he feels he was entitled to. In the present, may express his resentment against agency representatives and others for denial of his satisfactions by whiny complaints or, less frequently, by open attack.

11. <u>Dependency.</u> Attempts to use all others for gratification of infantile needs. Enormous, "bottomless pit" dependency. Indicates that the people he likes and continues to involve himself with are those who give him the material things he wants regardless of whether or not he returns the favor. May describe positive feelings about mother or other supportive (past) figures in terms of what they gave him. From time to time a complete verbal denial of dependency, often accompanied by non-verbal demands to be taken care of.

12. <u>No self-critical capacity.</u> Expresses no remorse about any of his behavior, past or present. No capacity to criticize his own past behavior.

13. <u>Impulsivity.</u> Behaves impulsively, blows up easily, reacts suddenly and violently on the basis of immediate

feelings even when there is no obvious evidence of stress or pressure. Cannot predict that others may react negatively to his behavior—or even that they may react at all.

14. <u>Poor control</u>. Characterized by poor impulse control, inability to bind tension, poor control of incoming stimuli, uncontrolled acting-out of hostility, inability to pursue goals in any meaningful or sustained way.

15. <u>No active attempts to intervene in life</u>. No apparent deliberate attempts (or attempts only of the crudest and most transparent sort) to bring about desired responses from the world. Attempts to manipulate or conform in an effort to get need satisfaction are minimal.

16. <u>Relationships with adults poor or non-existent</u>. Characterized by combination of resentment (or explosiveness) and dependency. Relationships with adults emotionally charged with both these feelings—may vacillate between the two. No real two-way (reciprocal) relationships with adults.

17. <u>Relationships with peers poor or non-existent</u>. Alienated. Relationships with peers characterized by demand and jealousy on his part and frequent scapegoating on the part of the peers.

18. <u>Primitive social techniques</u>. Techniques available to him are; automatic denial, transparently insincere and very clumsy efforts toward ingratiation, complaining, bullying, flight, and direct violence.

19. <u>Reasons for delinquency</u>. Delinquency may result from poor impulse control (wanting >taking; hating > physical attack; fear > flight) or inability to cope with external

pressures" ("used" by adults or peers in delinquent act, agitated by others into aggressive act).

Perceived as:

20. <u>By correctional workers</u>: Not criminalistic, but helpless, blundering, and very difficult to deal with in typical institution or field settings.

21. <u>By non-professional adults</u>; Unstable, unpredictable, immature, unteachable. Attempts to handle him by paternalistic exploitation or punitive behavior.

22. <u>By peers</u>; Odd, undependable, inappropriate, "loner," sometimes bullying, sometimes cowardly.

Differentiation among the I-2s:

23. Although I-2s have the above characteristics in common, they may also be differentiated on the following dimensions, which are relevant to treatment planning:

    A. Sensitivity to disapproval from others, I-2s range from apparent indifference to an extreme and constant set to look for criticism from others.

    B. Active-passive approach. I-2s vary in their tendencies to use active, but crude, attempts to bring about desired satisfactions; to use active attention-distracting devices (horseplay, etc.) to avoid relationships or response demands; or to use passive withdrawal.

    C. Nature of response to frustration or demand. Openly hostile attack, whining complaints, and obstinate refusal to accommodate - any of these responses may characterize a particular I-2.

These differentiating features combine in several ways in I-2s, so that the earlier (1961 version) division into subtypes Aggressive and Passive is not sufficiently complex. As more experience with I-2s is accumulated, subtype definitions will be presented.

My Supplemental Description

The following descriptions are based on many years of working with and observing the I-2. I have worked with them in nearly every possible social situation, controlled residential setting, in formal and informal outreach work, as a neighbor, friend, landlord and as a resident within my home. My observations are merely an addendum to the above description. I have found the I-Level Theory description accurately describes the I-2.

However, I don't necessarily agree that there are I-2 subtypes. I've found that all the symptoms described, as possible characteristics of different subtypes, can apply to all I-2s and are dependent on their environment at the moment and previous experiences with specific others.

The description of the I-2 isn't always apparent and the degree of the characteristic can vary some between I-2s. In various environments, situations, and relationships the symptoms can become manifest and quite apparent. The difficulty many have in discerning the limitations of the I-2, is due to the fact that I-2s are far more responsive to external stimuli than to any internal organized personality. They have very limited insight and foresight. Their behavior is dependent on their physical and social environment. They tend to identify with whomever they're associating with at the moment. If they're with "good guys" they act like a good guy. If with "bad guys" they act like a bad guy. When comfortable with the person they're with may, at the moment, verbalize some very mature and insightful conclusions and may even discuss some realistic goals, but, unfortunately, they are unable to internalize, or implement them. They require step-by-step, simple, supportive guidance.

His social functioning can be compared to that of a 3- to 7-year-old child. As such he requires the support and guidance of a 3- to 7-year-old child. He is described as being impulsive. The word "impulsive," I believe, needs a finer definition than normally assessed to it. Though synonymous with spontaneous, in respect to child behavior there appears to be a variation that requires defining. Spontaneity in a child is normally healthy behavior. Impulsivity gives the connotation that the child can predict the outcome, or the response to his behavior and with deliberate disregard for expectations or consequences, misbehaves. Without foresight this cannot be simple wanton behavior.

The I-2 is not motivated by a need for social acceptance but rather pleasure seeking. He seeks fun in each activity in which he is involved. He appears to have a short attention span, which is in reality a short interest span. As attested to by parents, when they find something they're interested in they can stay focused for prolonged periods. If the activity isn't fun, they lose interest in it.

Their violent acting out, for no reasonably apparent cause, can occur for various reasons. One may be as Spitz put it, *"Overstuffing has its parallel in over-stimulation, which may cause difficulties by flooding the psyche with stimuli faster than they can be comfortably handled."*

An adult I-2 related to me that in those moments everything seemed to be in a whirl. She became completely disoriented and lost all semblance of internal control. One youth I worked closely with, as an academic tutor, used the same method to express three different attitudes. One message was he wanted to tease me and make me think he was refusing to work. Another message was, "I just want to play." And still another was, "I really don't feel like working today." Though all three messages were communicated by the same behavior, I had to determine how to respond to each for the sake of the continuity of the treatment plan.

The frustration he demonstrates when not having his demands met appear to be the "spoiled brat" syndrome, but as many parents have found that simply giving him what he demands doesn't always satisfy him, or it only satisfies momentarily. I believe this phenomenon is caused by the fact that he doesn't really know what he needs, as is common with most people, but in his case he is neither able to speculate, nor communicate what he believes to be his real need. As with the child, mentioned above, he knew what he wanted, thought it was what he needed, but couldn't describe it specifically. From my interpretation, I chose to meet his real need with an appropriate response that was in keeping with the treatment strategy—strokes (sensory stimulation).

I found a parallel to this phenomena while working with geriatrics suffering from dementia, or Alzheimer's. When they would repeatedly ask the same question it would appear as though they were seeking information. But I found that is wasn't information they were seeking, but recognition. (See Berne.) By simply giving them a hug, a stroke on the back, or a kiss, the questions were discontinued, suggesting that it wasn't information but simply recognition, or stimulation, that they sought, but were unable to communicate their real need. I-2s are frequently criticized for their attention-getting behavior. Their need for sensory stimulation is so great that they need much attention. If they don't get it one way, they'll get it another. This need can be capitalized on with operant conditioning using physical contact as a generalized reinforcer.

They experience much stress in the presence of other persons. They are criticized, teased and generally abused so frequently that just the presence of others can be frightening. I-3 Mps are the most threatening. In fact the I-2 needs to be protected from the Mp. Most frequently, Mps deliberately go out of their way to antagonize I-2s, then when the I-2 reacts he is punished, while the Mp most frequently walks away as though innocent of any misdeed. They relate best to other I-2s and I-3 Cfms. Though I-2s, before treatment, may tend to fight a lot. It seems to be caused by a lack of knowing how else to relate. What may appear to be "hate" for his opponent can be contrasted when one or the other is hurting, or when separated for a time (as when one may be away on a furlough), with a real concern and worry for the seeming opponent.

They tend to bully and tease others. This is most commonly calculated; they rarely pick on someone who can defend himself or herself. On the other hand, I believe this may be influenced by experience. Young I-2s are known to challenge people much larger and obviously much stronger than they. As they grow older, and have taken a few beatings, they tend to be more passive and more discriminative in whom they challenge.

Many have multiple problems, which are difficult to manage due to their I-Level. Some have eidetic like perception. On a few occasions I've had them react to situations that occurred days before, and in one case, two years before, as though it had just occurred. In our Pioneer Lodge unit, it was common for the wards to know all the room numbers of the other twenty youths on the unit.

In the section dealing with treatment techniques, I will mention the effects of role reversal, which might have some eidetic perception implications.

Treatment of the I-2

In treating the I-2, the therapist must be fully aware of the I-2s potential. He cannot function as others of his chronological age. He has limited insight and foresight. Recall Point 4, on the undifferentiated view of others:

> *Since nothing exists for him except his own way*
> *of looking at things, he sees the actions of others as*

*arbitrary and unmotivated by feelings, each act
independent of any organized personality system.
Since he has no awareness of feelings in others, he
is unable to understand what others are doing to
him or what they expect of him. He shows little
agreement with others about reality.*

Treatment Plan for 1-2s:

1. <u>Goals</u>. Establish view of Agent as supportive, reduce
    pressure of asocial drives; develop some minimal
    measure of conformity by strengthening self control;
    increase ability to perceive relationship between needs
    (own and others) and behavior (own and others); protect
    from being scapegoated; reduce sense of isolation and
    rejection.

2. <u>Placement plan</u>. Consider a foster home, since own home
    can be expected to be difficult or impossible to work
    with, or may represent the source of the deprivation.
    Foster parents should be tolerant, able to behave tenderly,
    understanding of child's immaturity, able to establish
    simple concrete structure.

3. <u>Family variables</u>. Close work with foster parents to offer
    support in dealing with this frustrating, demanding,
    complaining and/or aggressive ward. Support may take
    the form of constant interpretation of youth's primitive
    needs and infantile reactions to denial. Illustrations in
    terms of behavior of small children are useful.

4. <u>Location of community supports</u>. Some person(s)
    or group must be found in the community (relative,
    foster parent, teacher, agency worker, policeman,
    Salvation Army) who can continue to provide a long-

term supportive relationship even beyond agency responsibility and control.

5. Job and school recommendations. If of job age, find job where ward works alone or has a minimum amount of frustrating interpersonal dealings; e.g., gardening, farm work, repetitive factory or food processing work. If of school age, clarify for teacher youth's ineptitudes, help predict youth's behavior, try to give perspective on youth's problem and on Agent's long-range treatment plan. Offer the employer or teacher support as with foster family.

6. Peer group and recreation variables. Needs to be protected from peer group scapegoating; encourage peers to take care of him. Activity group program to develop peer-relating capacities. Use of peers as props in role-playing with individual re-living, then reviewing, and real life experiences.

7. Kind of controls. Offer clear, unambiguous structure; demands should be simple and of a concrete, action nature; insistence on conformity should be gradual with no great penalties for early nonconformity.

8. Kind of agent. Tolerant, supportive, protective, instructive, dependable, calm in crisis, personally secure, non-threatened by inappropriate, primitive, "idinal" outbursts. Agent must be able to give structure and support rather than insight counseling. Must have ability to work with foster homes.

9. Agent attitudes. Focus not on the behavior but the cause. Supportive, constructive human relationship should be offered. Give personal interest, personal attention, recognition, credit and reward where appropriate. Do

not encourage extreme dependency because excessive demands cannot be met. Avoid self-pity sessions and projections of blame. Extremely slow progress, if any, toward recognizing the expectations of the real world is to be expected.

10. <u>Treatment methods</u>. Both individual and group procedures may be used in teaching: (1) awareness of own responses, (2) perception (and eventually prediction) of responses in others, (3) impact of individuals on each other, and (4) behavior techniques for dealing with environment.

An effective form of treatment with the I-2 is psychodrama, in which the ward acts out, rather than verbalizes, needs, feelings, interactions, and problem solving. Activity groups of I-2s may be used to develop peer relationships and to give the I-2, some pleasure and satisfaction in the activity itself.

Ward should not be "interviewed"—rather agent should go through daily life experiences with him. Traditional psychotherapy is not appropriate with the I-2; "guided growth" is appropriate.

11. <u>Suggested techniques for achieving treatment goals</u>. The Agent must clarify for the youth the meaning of specific behavioral acts—both his and those of important figures in his life. This may be achieved via psychodrama techniques, including role reversal, doubling, behind-the-back, acting out fantasy. Out-of-bounds aggressiveness must be limited in as matter-of-fact a manner as possible without allowing youth to interpret limits as hostility or rejection. Agent needs to be sensitive to evidences of tension, and to simplify demands or remove pressure during tension periods. Any tentative attempts at self

control or self-responsibility should be rewarded. Find opportunities for him to do something for others and reward with warm approval.

12. <u>Kind of help the Agent needs</u>. Agent needs help in understanding the dynamics of the case and help in dealing with the community pressures (the angry environment of the I-2). Provide much staff support for the Agent who must deal with the frustrations provided by this youth-- with his outbursts, accusations, withdrawals, demands for automatic gratification. Minimize pressure on the Agent (partially internal) for quick success with the I-2s. Provide Agent with a caseload, which contains change-of-pace cases (i.e., cases who are more responsive to the Agent as a person, have more potential for development, and possess the possibilities of quicker success).

13. <u>Questions.</u> What should the ultimate goal with an I-2 be? Should we be satisfied with a marginally-functioning individual in the community? Where should the ultimate agency responsibility lie?

Treatment Techniques: Relationship Building

Relationship building is of primary importance in treating the I-2. Initially he is not motivated by social acceptance; he is fun oriented. Because of their identification problem and their defensiveness, it is essential for the agent to be seen as a good guy—non-threatening and non-critical. Because the I-2 doesn't have an integrated identity, he identifies with whomever he is associated at the moment. If the agent is intimidating, he will get intimidation in return from the I-2. If he is seen as a loving, caring person, the I-2 will respond in a similar manner. Because of the I-2's sensitivity to criticism, the agent should avoid criticism, a raised voice, name-calling, anger and physical abuse. Doing so will only reinforce the very behavior he is trying to extinguish. The agent should look for the positive behavior of the

I-2 and reinforce it with compliments (symbolic strokes), or physical contact such as a pat on the back or a hug.

How the I-2 perceives the agent is primarily dependent on the congruency of the verbal and non-verbal communication of the agent, or perhaps just the non-verbal communication. I've sat in treatment team meetings where the leaders would say to the youth, "We care about you and we're here to help you," while the atmosphere was really hostile. The non-verbal communication was, "Either shape up kid or pay consequences." The I-2 reacts to the non-verbal cues; he becomes frightened and confused and either withdraws, or acts out.

When I first encounter an I-2, I greet him with a warm smile implying that he is a good person and I like him. With rare exception, I ask, "Do you like hugs?" Invariably I receive an affirmative answer, both from young and old I-2s alike. Immediately following the hug, I compliment them on giving great hugs. In doing this, I'm laying the groundwork for implementing "Operant and Respondent Conditioning." I'm creating a good guy image—a person who is willing to give him the attention he needs. It also meets his sensory need at the moment and defers acting out as a means to gain attention. He also learns that pleasing the agent can get his needs met, which is an initial step in building the relationship.

To develop the most productive relationship with an I-2 the agent must love young children, have a warm smile, a good sense of humor, like to play and laugh with young children, have much patience, and be able to appreciate and evaluate what the I-2's potential is. Like other personalities, each has his own individual potential. The primary goal of my treatment method is to enhance the I-2's ability to function under stress and to be able to function acceptably in his social environment. The I-2 can be one of the most loving and lovable children you'll ever meet. Without the appropriate care and guidance, he can be one of the most obnoxious, frustrating children you can meet.

There are those who work with the I-2 who make the erroneous assumption that this is "spoiling him." Nothing could be farther from the truth. With the appropriate conditioning the I-2 will spoil the agent. As the relationship develops the I-2 becomes motivated to please the agent. In the process he is learning more appropriate ways to relate and in turn increases his ability to function. However, regardless of how improved his interpersonal relationship skills become, he can never be expected to function as well as other personalities of his chronological age.

"The world should take care of him, but ordinarily doesn't do an adequate job. He does not perceive himself as needing to contribute anything." This statement is rather ambiguous. The term "giver or withholder" can be misconstrued to imply material desires rather than basic needs, i.e. food, shelter, clothing, nurturing, etc.

Bearing in mind the chapter on sensory stimulation, let us recall Berne:

> *The ability of the human psyche to maintain coherent ego states seems to depend upon a changing flow of sensory stimuli. This observation forms the psychobiological basis of social psychiatry. In structural terms, these stimuli are necessary in order to assure the integrity of the neopsyche and the archaeopsyche. If the flow is cut off or flattened into monotony, it is observed that the neopsyche gradually becomes disorganized ("The individual's thinking is impaired"); this lays bare the underlying archaeopsychic activity ("He shows childish emotional responses"); and finally archaeopsychic function becomes disorganized as well ("He suffers from hallucinations"). This is the sensory deprivation experiment.*

The work of Spitz goes a little farther. It demonstrates that sensory deprivation in the infant may result not only in psychic changes, but also in organic deterioration. This shows how vital it is for the changing sensory environment to be maintained. In addition, a new and specific factor appears: the most essential and effective forms of sensory stimulation are provided by social handling and physical intimacy. Hence Spitz speaks of "emotional deprivation" rather than of "sensory deprivation". The intolerance for long periods of boredom or isolation gives rise to the concept of stimulus-hunger, particularly for the kind of stimuli offered by physical intimacy. This stimulus-hunger parallels in many ways, biologically, psychologically, and socially, the hunger for food. Such terms as malnutrition, satiation, gourmet, gourmand, faddist, ascetic, culinary arts, and good cook are easily transferred from the field of nutrition to their analogues in the field of sensation. Over-stuffing has its parallel in over-stimulation, which may cause difficulties by flooding the psyche with stimuli faster than they can be comfortably handled. In both spheres, under ordinary conditions where ample supplies are available and a diversified menu is possible, choices will be heavily influenced by individual idiosyncrasies.

And as Fritz Perls stated:

> . . . the great thing to understand: that awareness per-se by and of itself-can be curative. Because with full awareness you become aware of this organismic self-regulation, you can let the organism take over without interfering, without

interrupting; we can rely on the wisdom of the organism. And the contrast to this is the whole pathology of self-manipulation, environmental control, and so on, that interferes with this subtle organismic self-control.

As I said, I agree with Perls. If the organism is aware of what is occurring, it is capable of correcting any conflicts. However, if they have dysfunctional, or impaired sensory receptors, the organism cannot perceive the stimuli and thus is unaware of any conflict, or its resolution.

Studies of SPD, (Sensory Processing Disorder) suggests that some people have a neurological problem that disables certain sensory receptors. The I-2 could well fit this category. However, I have focused on relationship building by use of respondent and operant conditioning using sensory stimulation as the reinforcer.

Consider the statement:

> *The work of Spitz goes a little further. It demonstrates that sensory deprivation in the infant may result not only in psychic changes, but also in organic deterioration. This shows how vital it is for the changing sensory environment to be maintained. In addition, a new and specific factor appears: the most essential and effective forms of sensory stimulation are provided by social handling and physical intimacy.*

Specific Treatment Techniques

Contrary to the I-Level description of the I-2, I found that they can develop relationships that are not materialistic. Where the I-Level Theory focuses on interpersonal relationships, I directed my efforts to help the I-2 develop a repertoire of skills, void of materialism, to improve his ability to relate to others.

In some cases, where I took over the care of an I-2 that had been previously treated with material gains, I gradually weaned them from expecting material gains to looking forward to our relationship. Given the opportunity and time (six to eight months), I was able to teach them to value relationships and increase their relationship building skills.

This was achieved by helping them succeed in performing various tasks, play activities, work and just plain association in activities of their choice. Destructive criticism, a raised voice, name-calling and excessive force when physical restraint is necessary were all avoided. I look for acceptable behavior and immediately reinforce it with sensory stimulation using generalized reinforcers such as hugs, pat on the back, or praise enthusiastically applied.

I had one difficult I-2, tell me, "You're the only one who sees the good things I do." His father testified that I was the only one that could manage him,

On one occasion he had refused to meet with his therapist. Through manipulative means they had, at least, got him to an area outside of the therapist's office. When I arrived to join him, I found him surrounded by several people who were trying to corral him into the therapist's office. I went to his father to find out what was happening. He explained that he was refusing to see his therapist and was being obstinate. I then approached him, and the father advised everyone else to back away. I greeted him and walked away to a spot seclusive of the others. He followed me, as I expected he would.

I then asked him what the problem was; why he didn't want to see his therapist. He told me that if he went inside to the therapist's office they would detain him and send him to a mental health facility. He explained that he didn't want any part of that. If his therapist wanted to talk to him she would have to come outside. I told him that I doubted very much that they wanted to send him to mental health, but I would talk to his therapist. I told him I couldn't promise whether I could get her to agree to come outside, but I did promise that I would do my best.

When I explained the situation to his therapist she agreed to meet him outside. She took him to a little secluded garden and had their discussion without further difficulty.

There were many subtle dynamics that preceded and occurred during this episode. This youth, a teenage I-2, as with most other I-2s, had only met with intimidation and coercion most of his life. His father was under pressure from his school, his case worker and other various agencies to make his son conform to their demands. Though the father sought the help of these agencies, none were able to provide appropriate information to enable the father to achieve their expectations.

My first encounter with this youth and his father was to transport and join them in a meeting with his school "treatment team" to discuss his school performance. I recognized that he was frightened in anticipation of the meeting. I attempted to reassure him and reduce his fear with both physical, (gentle touch), and symbolic strokes, (encouragement and expressions of care).

On my next contact I was to escort him to his therapist. I had arrived earlier than necessary to talk with he and his parents. After a few brief words to express interest in him, he left and went to a nearby park. Inasmuch as we still had ample time to make his appointment, I ignored his leaving and continued to talk with his parents until it was time to leave for his appointment. I then went to the park to pick him up and when he saw me he ran to the car and said that he was just trying to call me on a cell phone. He got in the car and we proceeded to his therapist.

In incidents such as this, more often than not, the authority figure will get anxious and respond authoritatively. In such instances, the authority will meet with counter aggression in the form of an argument or simply refusal to meet his appointment, which in turn can gain the attention of the authority person and thus meet his sensory needs. In this case, I immediately reinforced his arrival at the car with a complement and a stroke on the back. This served multiple purposes. It reinforced his appropriate response, supported our relationship and met his sensory need thus deferring any need for aggressive behavior. This was also an example of "successive approximation."

My intent was to improve his interpersonal relationship skills, improve his responses to authority requests and at the same time improve his self esteem and reduce his aggressiveness. Though he never directed any aggressive behavior towards me, he demonstrated his aggressive behavior, both passive and active, in the academic setting. In the academic setting they were reinforcing the very behavior they were trying to extinguish. They used intimidation and coercion to motivate him. Though, in a relatively short time, we developed a positive relationship; he would respond to my requests without any difficulty. Had he been treated with the same positive reinforcement, he would have responded as well there.

Principles of Shaping New Behavior

Let's review what we know:

There are two aspects in shaping skillful behavior: (a) reinforcing only certain responses, which is called (1) differential reinforcement; and (b) gradually raising the requirement for reinforcement, which is called (2) successive approximations.

In differential reinforcement, one form of behavior is reinforced and other, possibly rather similar, forms are not reinforced.

It is more than simple conditioning when we differentially reinforce successive approximations to a final form of behavior. When we follow the procedure, we are said to be shaping behavior.

Complex skills must be shaped very gradually. As the criterion for differential treatment is shifted, successive approximations to the final behavior are made.

In shaping any given behavior, we gradually changed the criterion of what to reinforce. The desired behavior is approached by successive approximations.

For best results in shaping behavior, the conditioned reinforcer should be presented in a close temporal relation to the response.

Another example of shaping behavior occurred when I began working at the Fricot School. Every Saturday our 8- to 12-year-old youths had to clean their rooms and the living unit, and pass a rather stringent inspection. Following the inspection, the youths were taken on a hike and provided with a bag lunch at their destination. Those that didn't pass the inspection had to remain in the Head Group Supervisor's office until the others returned.

One youth, a rather slovenly one, had repeatedly failed his inspection. On this particular day he had completely given up even trying. I encouraged him to at least make an attempt. When the inspector arrived, I asked him to pass this youth no matter how bad his room was. The Inspector agreed and told the youth his room wasn't too bad and he had passed. I then reinforced his effort with sensory stimulation. The following week he was more eager to make the effort to clean his room. Though it still didn't meet the desired criterion, it was an improvement over the previous week and was reinforced accordingly. This process was repeated every week. Each week there was progressive improvement in both his effort and his results. After a few weeks, encouragement was no longer needed. He willingly made the effort and met the criterion to pass. This was the result of reinforcing successive approximations related to his effort and his results. The task became the stimulus and the achievement became the reinforcer.

In the case of another youth, I was to tutor him with his homework. He was illiterate and attended a "special ed" class. He was a 9-year-old I-2 youth. During my initial interview with he and his grandparents, I used my usual approach, "Do you like hugs?"

As expected, he responded in the affirmative. His sisters, younger and older, were also present, so, hugs were passed out all around. This gave me a preferred status with the whole family. Following my interview, after arranging the times and purposes of my assignment, hugs were given out, all around again, as I left.

On the following week, when I arrived for our first tutoring session, the kitchen table had been cleared for a work place. I began with my usual hug. This was to continue the development of our relationship and to avert the need to act out for attention (sensory stimulation).

When we began to work on his lesson, ten spelling words to be written ten times each. He said, "I don't want to work." He then attempted to get up from the table and run away, his usual behavior. I restrained him, using only the minimum amount of force necessary and maintaining my composure.

At this point, I was attempting to create a working area. As Skinner pointed out: *"Pigeon C's record does not reveal the speed of acquiring a key pecking response because other processes are also involved. The pigeon must first adapt to the box and the click. Conditioning can occur very fast when adaptation is already complete and when each response is immediately reinforced."*

Before any real progress could be made toward achieving the task at hand, this youth had to adapt to several contingencies. The restraint was used as a method for reinforcing avoidance behavior. When he sat at the table preparing for work, the restraint was removed. By sitting at the table preparing for work he was avoiding the restraint. When he sat at a table preparing for work he was immediately reinforced with a generalized reinforcer; a stroke on the back and praise recognizing his appropriate behavior. He repeated, "I don't want to work."

This was met with a technique known as role reversal. Role reversal is a very rapid and effective technique, but it must be administered in very specific ways, if not it most often backfires. The I-2 is usually admonished for his statement and most frequently an argument ensues. If you find yourself arguing with an I-2, or I-3, you've been had. He is controlling you rather than the alternative. In role reversal you don't mock or make fun of the client; you join him.

I said, "Okay, we'll just sit here." We sat there and did nothing.

He continued to struggle to escape. At the same time, while restraining him I was also stroking his back. He then said to me, "You're stronger than my last tutor." When he decided that his struggling was futile he decided to try a manipulative technique common to I-2s. He began a whiny type of crying so I joined him (role reversal). After many minutes of the crying I said, "This is no fun what else can we do? Let's arm wrestle." That lasted for a few minutes, but we remained sitting at the table doing nothing.

After, about an hour, I said, "This is no fun. Let's do the work and get it over with."

He thought about that for a minute and then said, "Let's do it and get it over with." The assignment was completed in about fifteen minutes.

Doing the work was once again reinforcing avoidance behavior. However, he was immediately reinforced with the generalized reinforcers of sensory stimulation as soon as he made the effort to do the work, and repeatedly so as he progressed through the assignment.

Getting him to work for fifteen minutes was an accomplishment. I used continuous reinforcement initially. Each effort and accomplishment, no matter how slight, was reinforced with generalized reinforcers such as physical stroke, compliment and encouraging words.

Our second session was similar to the first. Some restraint was needed initially, but he soon settled down and concluded, "Let's do it and get it over with."

Initially his work was pretty sloppy. Doing a neater job became a second goal. I also wanted to extend his work time and hoped to teach him to read. He clearly stated, "I don't want to read! I hate to read!"

By the third session, he had adapted to the work area and our relationship had developed to the point where he looked forward to my arrival. He was also striving to please me. His grandfather testified, at a meeting of parents with difficult children, that he was elated over his grandson's progress. Where the grandson had only been getting 50% on his spelling scores, he was now getting 100% in just a matter of four weeks.

This had been achieved by the application of positive reinforcement; operant conditioning. I consistently maintained my patience and composure. I never raised my voice, got angry, called him names, or used excessive force to restrain him. We also had a lot of fun in the process; teasing each other yet remaining on track for our goals. I looked for the slightest positive progressive increments that approached the desired results and reinforced them with the generalized reinforcers previously described. (Successive approximations vs. punishment).

After a few weeks I had changed from continuous reinforcement to intermittent reinforcement.

He progressed from simply writing his spelling words to more complex word recognition assignments and some math. Initially, getting him to work for fifteen minutes was an accomplishment. After a few months, his work period was extended to an hour or more. The assignment had become the stimulus and the achievement the reinforcer.

I believed he had the potential to read. His grandmother, an illiterate, had been stressing phonics. I tried using phonics flash cards to determine his degree of understanding word structures. He seemed to understand the principles of phonics, but didn't seem to understand word fragments and their association with words.

He was doing well with his school assignments, so I decided to take him to the public library every other session. There I would select an easy book that I might read to him, and I also allowed him to select a book of his choice. I hoped that this might encourage an interest in reading. The library also had computers, some of which had educational games. I found a game that dealt with word fragments.

He figured out how to play the game faster than I did, but he saw it as a toy with lots of buttons to press. It was a fun thing to him. By this time we had a very great relationship. I had to struggle with him for control of the mouse, realizing this was a time of teasing. But I maintained control and turned it into a great learning experience.

He learned about word fragments and how they were used but still denied the ability to read.

One day I printed a few simple sentences on some construction paper and then cut the sentences into narrow strips. I then cut out each word providing several words on strips approximately 3/4 inch by 1 1/2". I took the strips and laid them in random order for the boy to read. He said, "Those words are easy!" And proceeded to read them with ease. I then reorganized the words into their original sentences and directed him to read the words again. He read the sentences with ease and we both got excited. "You can read!" He immediately ran to his grandmother and excitedly told her he could read.

Overtly, it appeared I had taught him to read. Such was not the case. His refusal to read was an identity problem. As mentioned in the description of the I-2, it states that he doesn't have an integrated personality of his own. That the I-2 identifies with whomever he is with at the moment. In this case he was identifying with his grandmother, who was an illiterate. His identity was related to the identity of his grandmother. Therefore, if grandmother was illiterate, he had to be illiterate to have an identity.

The following semester he was removed from the "special ed" program and placed in regular school classes. In later contacts with the grandfather, he reported his grandson was doing well in the regular school classes. Schoolwork had become the stimulus and the achievement the reinforcer. In the process, his self-esteem improved as well as his responses to his grandparents requests.

This youth only got angry at me once. He was having difficulty explaining to me the teacher's expectations for a special assignment. In his frustration at my inability to fully understand the project, he raised his voice and became even less comprehensible. I calmly pointed out to him that I did not yell at him and he had no need to yell at me. I also explained that I couldn't understand him when he yelled. I then told him to relax and try to explain to me again. He settled down and became more fluent and succeeded in explaining to me.

Tantrums

I-2s are noted for their frequent tantrums. In working with them I found they had two different types of tantrums or there were two different causes for the tantrums. One is often referred to as the "spoiled brat syndrome." The other is as Spitz describes: *"Overstuffing has its parallel in over-stimulation, which may cause difficulties by flooding the psyche with stimuli faster than they can be comfortably handled."*

As I mentioned in the description of the I-2, an adult I-2 related to me that in those moments everything seemed to be in a whirl. She became completely disoriented and lost all semblance of internal control. This is an example of the effects of excessive amounts of adrenaline.

Let's now discuss tantrums. Skinner refers to tantrums in terms of placating the demands of a child. He wrote:

> *The receipt of candy as a result of "throwing a tantrum" is an example of positive reinforcement. When the mother placates the child with candy and the child ceases to scream, both mother and child are, perhaps unknowingly, reinforcing each other's behavior. If termination of a temper tantrum reinforces a mother's response of giving candy to her child, the cessation of noise is an example of negative reinforcement. To avoid conditioning temper tantrums, the mother should not reinforce such behavior when it is emitted. If temper tantrums have been previously condition, the mother can*

extinguish the response by consistently not reinforcing it. When a temper tantrum results in the receipt of candy, the probability that the child will have a tantrum in the future increases. In addition to extinguishing temper tantrums, a mother may frequently reinforce "playing quietly." This would help to eliminate the tantrums by conditioning behavior which is incompatible with them.

In this case consistency by the mother is absolutely necessary if she's ever to extinguish the tantrums. Giving in once in a while merely reinforces behavior using an intermittent reinforcement schedule, which in turn makes it strongly extinction-resistant.

In the case of a tantrum resulting from over stimulation, we have two factors to consider. One, the psyche is unable to handle the incoming stimuli thus causing the child to become disoriented and confused and consequently frightened, emitting the "activation syndrome." In the activation syndrome, the hormone called adrenaline releases sugar into the blood from the liver. In fear or anger, secretion of adrenaline is elicited from the adrenal gland. In the activation syndrome, the blood is richly supplied with sugar and oxygen which are carried to muscle tissue more quickly by the increased pulse rate. If the amount of adrenaline is excessive, it can go so far as to induce a catatonic-like seizure, causing the muscles to get tense and even draw the body into a fetal position.

Adrenaline is commonly used by athletes to increase their proficiency. Occasionally, an athlete will get angry and produce an excessive amount of adrenaline reducing his efficiency. The trained athlete, through experience, learns to control the flow of adrenaline to maintain his maximum efficiency.

The I-2 seems unable to make these discretions. He gets excessive amounts of adrenaline causing completely uncontrollable tantrums. There may be a biological problem that causes the excesses of adrenaline. However, the I-2, as with the trained athlete, can learn to control the flow of adrenaline and thus maintain reasonable composure for the circumstances.

In working with I-2s I found that they can be conditioned to control the flow of adrenaline. In my section on sensory stimulation, I referred to some assertions of Fritz Perls, that each organism has a balance point which it is constantly striving to maintain. His statement concludes thus: *"Any disturbance of the organismic balance constitutes an incomplete gestalt, an unfinished situation forcing the organism to become creative, to find means and ways to restore that balance."*

In his book, *In and Out of the Garbage Pail*, Perls describes an incident where a symphonic violinist, with aspirations to become a soloist, was referred to him because his hand would cramp up when doing a solo, but not when in the orchestra. Perl's observations led him to believe it was due to an imbalance of the organism. He had the man change his body position while doing a solo. This man had been to many therapists in a period of ten years without success. In taking Perls advise, he suddenly found that he could play the solos through without his hand cramping up.

Shortly after I read this, I was confronted by an I-2 who had become frustrated by a task he was trying to perform. He became angry and began to have a catatonic-like seizure. His body was drawing into a fetal position. I told him to put his arms down and relax. (I had a good working relationship with him and he responded to my requests reasonably well.) As soon as he responded by lowering his arms, he was able to relax and regain his composure. In as much as the adrenaline caused his body to tense up, I assumed that changing the body position could influence the adrenaline flow, which it did.

In relation to Perls' statement that *any disturbance of the organisms balance can force the organism to find a means to restore that balance,* pure speculation suggests that perhaps the I-2 finds that by dissipating all available adrenaline restores the organisms balance. This can also suggest the I-2 does not know how to control the flow of adrenaline.

I decided to see if I could condition the I-2 to respond to key phrases that might help them control their tantrums caused by the overstimulation described by Spitz, and subsequently the excessive flow of adrenaline. Initially, most had to be restrained when having a seizure. While restraining them, I would gently stroke them and calmly tell them to relax. As soon as they relaxed, it was usually after they became exhausted and the adrenaline flow had ceased, I immediately reinforced the relaxed position with the generalized reinforcers previously described. I've used this method with I-2s whose ages range from two years old to young adults. It proved to be effective in each case, for me, in just a few reinforcements. All I had to do was to say "relax" and the tantrum would cease.

I was never able to observe others using the same key phrases. However, there was one youth I had treated when he was eight years old. I hadn't seen him for many years. He had been returned to the institution where I was working at the time. He was there under a special provision for I-2s. If they had difficulty in the community, their parole officers had the authority to place them in an institution for up to thirty days. He wasn't placed on my unit. He was sixteen years old at the time. One day, while visiting a youth in the isolation unit, I heard someone throwing a tantrum from one of the isolation rooms. The minute I heard it I knew exactly who the culprit was. No one could throw a tantrum like he could. He had ceased to have them when he was on my unit. But, I'm afraid, returning to his previous environment merely reinforced the tantrums again. I went to the door of the room he was in and used the same key phrase I had used eight years before. He immediately stopped acting out and calmed right down. Though the tantrums hadn't been completely extinguished, the conditioned response was still intact.

The sequence of events in the process of shaping the I-2s behavior began with an aversive stimulus, restraint. When he calmed down and relaxed, he was released, thus reinforcing avoidance behavior. However, this was paired with the generalized reinforcers described and the word "relax" (or any other key word, or phrase that the therapist might choose). This was done calmly in acceptance of the tantrum. In a relatively short time, in just two, or three reinforcements, in some cases one time, the youth began to respond to the key word. At first, only part way through the tantrum, but gradually the key phrase could halt the tantrums almost immediately. I had paired the word "relax" with the means to escape restraint. In conditioning the body to relax, the body's position changed, thus reducing the flow of adrenaline and bringing the organism back into the balance it sought.

In some cases where the "spoiled brat syndrome" has been reinforced, but not yet extinguished, the I-2 may act out in the same manner as a child suffering from over stimulation. He may get violent and destructive. In this case, the same methods used for the overstimulated youth may be employed. Bringing the organism back into balance by reducing the flow of adrenaline enables the child to respond more rationally.

In essence, this procedure follows the suggestion of Skinner, reinforcing relaxing is incompatible with a tantrum.

Role Reversal

In describing the methods I used with the young I-2 I tutored, who didn't want to work, I mentioned "role reversal." This is another method I've found useful in extinguishing tantrums. This method is especially effective with the I-2.

I can't explain the dynamics involved but the method has invariably worked for me. In role reversal you are joining the I-2 in the behavior pattern that you hope to extinguish. You do exactly as he is doing. It's not used to mock, tease, or ridicule him. If you do, it will, most often, backfire and only aggravate the I-2. You must be a good actor and be able to mimic exactly what he's doing. You're not mocking him but you're joining him. When used appropriately, the behavior is immediately extinguished. Like I said, I don't understand how or why it works, but it works.

When working at the Fricot Ranch School, with the I-2 unit, we had a youth who was probably the most difficult to work with in the entire CYA. When I had only been there a few days, I was marching the boys to the dining room and out of a clear blue sky he began cussing me and calling me all sorts of names, some new. I did the same thing to him using exactly the same words, same attitude, same tone of voice, etc. He never did it again.

In addition to this episode, he used to throw tantrums continuously. He was so disruptive in the classroom that the teacher made a playpen for him. When he was initially tested, he was diagnosed as having borderline intelligence. All possible means were attempted to constrain him. One day when he was throwing a tantrum in the dayroom, he was on the floor kicking his feet and pounding his fist. I lay down beside him without saying a word and began doing the same thing. Of course, I was doing all I could to restrain myself from laughing. I thought the eyes of the other youths were going to fall out, or their jaws were going to drop to their toes. I had them convinced that I was actually having a tantrum. After just a few minutes of this, the one throwing the tantrum looked at me and grinned broadly. That was the last time he threw a tantrum like that.

A few weeks later, he was mad and went to his room and began trashing it. He was throwing everything he could get his hands on. So I entered his room and joined him. As I was throwing items, I picked up one item that he didn't want thrown. He said, "Not that!" I said, "Okay" and grabbed another item and asked if it was okay. He said, "Yeah."

After a few minutes he became exhausted, broke down in tears and came to me for a hug. I gave him a hug and let him sob for a while. When he calmed down, I told him to wash his face, straighten up his room and come back out to the dayroom. He meekly agreed and did exactly as he was asked. He never threw one of those room trashings again.

This finally culminated when we were in the dining room line one time. I corrected him for doing something. I don't remember what it was, but he got mad, pulled back his fist as though to attack. At the time I was carrying the unit roster, which was attached to a clipboard that had been remodeled with a piece of 3/4" plywood. Sticking with role reversal, I pulled back that board as though I was going to hit him (I don't know what I would've done if he had called my bluff).

He stood there with his fist cocked for several minutes. He gave serious thought to that clipboard, put his fist down and never repeated that act.

I've used this same method with other I-2s and it still amazes me how effective it is. You must be a good actor and genuinely appear to be joining them. Anything less can be a disaster.

In the case of this youth, after a short while in our program, was re-tested and found to have an IQ of 126. Though he started out as pre-schooler in a playpen, by the time he was sixteen he had graduated from high school.

Arguing

Earlier I said that if you find yourself in an argument with an I-2, or an I-3, you've been had. In the case of the I-2 this can serve two purposes:

1. Manipulation to have his demands met.

1. To maintain your attention to meet his sensory needs.

To be caught in an argument only reinforces contentious behavior. By stating the facts, turning and walking away is negative reinforcement of arguing; attention from the agent is withdrawn. The child is seeking sensory stimulation in an inappropriate way. In my experiences I've found that the child will follow me, then use a more appropriate way to gain my attention. This behavior is immediately reinforced with a stroke. Thus the contentious behavior is being extinguished while the appropriate, incompatible behavior is being reinforced.

Blundering

Due to their blundering tendencies and their many interpersonal relationship difficulties, they are constantly criticized, ridiculed, physically abused, teased, exploited, etc. Though they sincerely want to please others, they tend to recognize that they just don't know how; too many times they are criticized for their results and too little praise and support for their efforts and intent.

The I-2's social functioning can be compared to that of a 3- to 7-year-old child. As such, he requires the support and guidance of a 3- to7-year-old child. As young children enjoy repeated activities, such as having their favorite book read to them repeatedly and their favorite games repeatedly played, etc. when compared to spontaneous activities, they are better able to anticipate the ending. In the case of the I-2 where they have so many failures, repetitious successes are essential for their well-being. Activities are better selected for their success potential rather than simply affording a new experience.

They often frustrate others who attempt to appeal to their intellect to resolve any unreasonable demands. They can be conditioned to respond to "No" with a simple explanation in a non-threatening relationship. Diverting their attention is another technique for avoiding confrontation, always accompanied with stroking.

They can verbalize some very realistic insightful conclusions. They can also quote many insightful conclusions that they have heard. However, due to their limited internalized insight and foresight they are seldom able to successfully implement even the simplest of plans. This is why they are most frequently seen as blunderers. For this very reason it is rare, if ever, that they can succeed in independent living. Throughout their lives they are dependent on others for guidance and support. There are some who have succeeded in independent living and have been able to maintain certain occupations, but in each instant there have been supporting figures assisting them. Their intellect also plays an important factor in enabling them to succeed. Some are very bright while others are not.

The I-2 is best treated with respondent and operant conditioning.

CHAPTER 2

The I-3

Ways of Perceiving the World:
1. <u>Social Perception Deficiencies</u>. Minimum differentiation. The world and people in it dichotomized in black/ white fashion. His <u>under</u> estimation of the personality and behavioral differences among others and of the complexity of others both contribute to his deficiency in accurately predicting the response of others to him, as well as to his overconfidence in his prediction ability.

2. <u>Concern with Power Fields</u>. Perceives the world and his role in it on a power dimension. This is primary interpersonal concern.

3. <u>Searches for Structure</u>. Seeks structure in terms of rules and formulas for operation. Wants to know exactly what structure (system) to expect, who the power is, etc. Is more comfortable when the external structure is clearly defined and consistent. In searching, he is not looking for new information, but rather attempting to fit incoming information into pre-existing structures.

4. <u>No Internalized Value System</u>. Behaves not on the basis of some inner value system but rather on the basis of whatever external code of the moment has the support of power behind it. No internalized guilt - does not hurt inside when he violates the code he is following at the time. May make superficial protestations of guilt on request or to serve his own ends.

5. <u>Problems as External</u>. Problems are the result of conflicts between himself and some aspect of his environment. Not aware of any internal conflicts. Uncomfortable with idea of change in himself or living situation. Primarily feels that others' behavior should change and, as a result, his problems will then be reduced.

6. <u>Unable to Empathize with Others</u>. Cannot put himself in another's shoes. Although he may have learned or can learn to play a few stereotyped roles, he cannot understand the individualized needs, feelings and motives of another person who is different from himself.

7. <u>Cognitively Concrete</u>. Thinking and learning processes are highly concrete. Does not spontaneously compare, noting similarities and differences. Little motivation for integrating, interpreting, abstracting or resolving information. This may result in non-congruence between generalizations and specific behavior. Does not deal in levels of meaning or alternate meanings.

8. <u>Self Definition</u>. Self-definition has a restricted range of content with regard to positive and negative characteristics. At a conscious level, he is unambivalent regarding "who he is" and regarding whether or not he measures up to expectations. Conscious self-judging or

self-evaluating aspects are avoided, and appear to be virtually absent.

9. <u>Low Self Esteem</u>. Basically, does not think of himself as a worthwhile person. This general evaluation of self may be very close to consciousness (as in the Cfm) or actively defended against in an effort to feel strong and in control (as in the Mp and Cfc).

Ways of Responding to the World:

10. <u>Formulas for Operation</u>. Assumes that a very few rules, formulas, or techniques will handle interpersonal interaction. Makes efforts to manipulate his environment to bring about "giving" rather than "denying" response, so that his wishes and/or needs will be met and his fears evaded. May manipulate by conning, conforming, or intimidating.

11. <u>Description of Others Stereotyped and Nondynamic</u>. Describes others only in terms of the role they play in life (mother, supervisor, vice principal) or in terms of stereotyped "popular" responses (fathers are hard-working, mothers are nice, supervisors are strict or lenient). No dynamic or individualized descriptions of others, others' needs and feelings are assumed to be the same as his own.

12. <u>Impunitive</u>. Without cue or demand there is little spontaneous assessment of blame for past and present difficulties and failures. On cue or demand for assessment of guilt, may verbally blame self, or "bad companions", or may say "people who were messing-over me". This is usually followed by justifying or minimizing any active, personal involvement.

13. <u>Short-Term Planning</u>. When he plans, it is all for the immediate situation. Tries hard to work things out so that he will be comfortable right now without worrying much about tomorrow. Unmotivated to achieve in a long-range sense. Unmotivated to plan in detail for the future.

My Supplemental Description

In view of many years of observing I-3s in both controlled residential settings as well as a variety of field settings, the behavior patterns of each of the I-3 types are virtually identical. This suggests a genetic factor, as has been found in studies of identical twins. Though there are effective techniques for re-shaping the behavior of Cfcs and Cfms, Mps are far more difficult and considered incurable. However, in a controlled residential setting, utilizing an intensive therapeutic environment, it was found that their behavior and aggressiveness, both passive and active, dramatically changed. This suggests that their behavior per se was not genetically determined but another characteristic hampers their sensitivity, or awareness, of their physical and social environment. Though each of the three types have their own unique behavior patterns all have similar insensitivity to their environment.

From Perl's book, *Gestalt Verbatim,* I quote:

> ...the most important, interesting phenomenon in all pathology: self -regulation. The anarchy which is usually feared by the controllers is not an anarchy which is without meaning. On the contrary, it means the organism is left alone to take care of itself, without being meddled with from outside. And I believe that this is the great thing to understand: that awareness per se - by

and of itself - can be curative. Because with full
awareness you become aware of this organismic
self-regulation, you can let the organism take
over without interfering, without interrupting;
we can rely on the wisdom of the organism. And
the contrast to this is the whole pathology of self
manipulation, environmental control, and so on,
that interferes with this subtle organismic self-
control (p. 16).

The awareness that Perls speaks of, I believe to be a valid statement,
regarding persons with the insight necessary for awareness. However,
I-3s seem unable to realize the significance of their physical and
social environment due to dysfunctional sensory receptors. If the
sensory stimuli don't fall within the thresholds of their receptors,
there is no awareness, and therefore no response. In as much as the
behavior patterns of each of the I-3 types are virtually identical as
others of the same type, this suggests a genetic factor is involved.
In tracing the genealogy of I-3s, I found each to have the same
genealogy; that is, each were the progeny of an Mp. The Mp is noted
for his insensitivity, which will be discussed further in the section
relating to the treatment strategy for the Mp.

CHAPTER 3

The I-3 Cfc

From the 1965 edition, here are the characteristics:

Ways of Perceiving the World:

1. <u>Satisfied with Mode of Living - Resists Change</u>. Gives overall impression of feeling that his way of life is comfortable, effective and satisfactory. Rejects the idea of change in himself, his attitudes, and situations. Problems, if admitted, are minimized and are not internal struggles, but rather represent conflicts between him and some aspect of the external world (school, for example). His "mistakes" (problems with the law) are in the past.

2. <u>Self Concept as a "Generator" of Response in Others</u>. Overestimates the potential of his formula (surface conformity) as a means of being able to control others and bring about the desired outcome in any situation. Feels he has to "do something" to "turn the world on".

3. <u>Concern with Personal Consistency</u>. Uncomfortable when he perceives inconsistencies in presentation of himself to others. May make an effort to handle discrepant information. Does not condemn himself in situations where he does not comply fully with his self-image, but does feel somewhat uncomfortable following such non-compliance.

4. <u>Anti-Social Behavior Not Ego-Alien</u>. Comfortable with "delinquent" self-label. Delinquent acts are an acceptable part of the self-image and may be defended against criticism so that behavior appears warranted, reasonable and justified. Anti-social behavior seen simply as meeting one's own needs or the needs of one's own group, reacting appropriately to a rejecting society.

5. <u>Nature of Crisis</u>. Anxiety arises when formula for operating fails to work with authority figure or with peer group. For example, when Cfc is faced simultaneously with authority and peer system, he cannot "conform" to both.

6. <u>Rejection of Adults</u>. Has given up on satisfying relationships with adults. Perceives adults as being unable or unwilling to meet his dependency needs. Does perceive peers as being able to meet these needs.

7. <u>Self Description in Conventional Terms</u>. Describes himself initially as "average", "normal", "just like everyone else". Presents himself as relatively strong and in control of himself.

8. <u>Others in Terms of His Own Needs and Feelings</u>. His perceptions of others' motivations are similar to that he sees in himself. No awareness that individual needs and feelings different from his own exist. For

example, believes that all individuals act, not on the basis of internal need, but only on the basis of external structure.

9. <u>Anxiety Situational.</u> Anxiety related to environmental factors (e. g. , anticipation of environmental threat, lack of structure, caught in middle of opposing demands from adults and peers, unclear expectations) rather than a function of internal conflict. May be situationally anxious when undergoing a new experience. This anxiety is concerned with how to behave in a situation for which a ready formula is not available.

Ways of Responding to the World:

10. <u>Rigid Application of Formulas.</u> Use of formulas tends to be rigid, indiscriminate, stereotyped and absolutistic. Differential application of rules because of individual differences or because of situational differences is minimal. Has a primitive ability to apply two or three simple formulas; for example, may respond to some authorities in terms of their need to control and to others in terms of their need to help. May use somewhat different techniques in handling policeman and social worker.

11. <u>Conformity to Specific Reference Group.</u> Gravitates toward delinquently-oriented peer-group since his past history makes this group most knowable, most predictable to him. Tends to restrict his need for social approval to this group when possible. However, behaviorally complies with authority power structure when this is unavoidable. In an institutional setting, may tend to "melt into the walls", "be lost in the crowd".

12. <u>Relationships with Others Superficial and Short-Lived</u>. Does not have "close" relationships with others. Important to him to have companions but the specific individuals who fill this role are not crucial to him. Companion not chosen for their personal characteristics but rather by juxtaposition and/or signs of delinquent subculture belongingness (e.g., clothing, haircut, lingo)

13. <u>Reasons for Delinquency</u>. Offense behavior has one or more of the following meanings : Attempt to gain or maintain peer acceptance (masculinity proving), gratification of material needs, and defiance of adults

14. <u>Rejection of Emotionality</u>. Cannot handle (discuss) emotionally loaded material regarding family and own feelings. Deals with feelings by denial or joking. Describes himself as non-emotional and easygoing.

Treatment Plan for I-3 CFC:
(1966 Revision)

1. <u>Goals</u>. Reduce fear of close, non-superficial relationships with others, and of more direct expression of dependency needs; help Cfc form a more accurate cause-and-effect connection between his own behavior and the response of others to him; help him accept the legitimacy of the adult authority system; change self-definition in direction of non-delinquency personal worth, adequacy, maturity; increase social perceptiveness and prediction ability; increase interpersonal relating capacity.

2. <u>Placement Plan</u>. Cfcs can usually be placed with own family or with relatives. Characteristics of a satisfactory placement are: clear external structure,

open communication with the Treatment Agent, honest attempts on the part of the parents or substitutes to be supportive and understanding as well as limiting and realistically demanding, immediate action can be taken.

3. <u>Family Variables</u>. Agent should define "good parent" image to parents or substitutes as demonstrating concern for the Cfc (rather than rejection or indifference) by imposing clear external structure. Encourage parents to handle Cfc's behavior directly and immediately in firm, realistic and warm manner. Encourage parents to report to the Agent treatment-relevant behavior and attitudes on the part of the Cfc. Agent should support the Cfc in discussing attitudes of rejection or indifference in the home, without focusing blame on the parents. Agent should attempt to enhance the role or value of the Cfc's same sex parent, in cases where the parent is present. Formal family group therapy does not appear appropriate.

4. <u>Location of Community Supports.</u> Typically, the Cfc is not welcome in local programs because of his comfort with a delinquent label. As this label changes in treatment, Cfc may be encouraged to participate in any organization which will increase his feelings of worth and which relates to his abilities or interests - recreational, athletic or artistic. Cfc's family should be helped to locate community resources and agent should communicate with social agencies involved.

5. <u>Job and School Recommendations.</u> Some Cfcs are able to succeed in school and to hold a job successfully. Cfc will function best in highly structured class or job situation. Agent should verify school or job attendance. He should communicate with school counselor, dean or

employer so that misbehavior is known to Agent. If Cfc is unable to achieve in school, tutoring or continuation school may be a substituted.

6. <u>Peer Group and Recreation Variables</u>. Cfc typically has an acquaintance with many delinquent peers with whom he is comfortable (knows what to expect from them) but not close. Agent should build a Project peer group, composed of all Cfcs (first choice or Cfcs and Mps), which will support group members' non-delinquent behavior, non-delinquent attitudes, and eventually acceptance of the legitimacy of the adult authority system. Agent should support Cfc in following up on any recreational interests he may have; these are often in the area of noncompetitive sports such as weight-lifting. To the extent possible, activities should aim at alleviating cultural deprivation.

7. <u>Kind of Controls</u>. Cfc should first learn that someone can and will control him. A communication network set up around the Cfc (family, school, employer) can provide the Agent with the information necessary to control him. External structure should be well defined with penalties for unacceptable behavior also well-defined. Restrictions of his activities, use of extra work programs, and use of temporary detention are all useful in helping the Agent to communicate a message of <u>concern</u> for the Cfc.

8. This is 8. <u>Agent Characteristics</u>. Agent should have the ability to empathize on the basis of nonverbal modes of communication and to utilize nonverbal modes in conveying empathy, and the ability to be aware of primitive drives and defenses against these. Agent should have the ability to exert friendly but firm parental control, ability to act promptly and appropriately in

order to provide controls, ability to make definitive decisions and to act upon them. Agent should be able to understand the dependency needs underlying the "distance" facade. He should be able to accept and like the Cfc while he disapproves (and is willing to punish for) the misbehavior When the Cfc "hears" the Agent's message of concern and comes to the Agent, wanting to relate as child to parent, the Agent must be emotionally available.

9. <u>Treatment Methods</u>. Group treatment, with emphasis on current interpersonal dealings and techniques for staying out of trouble rather than on past history and reason (dynamics) for behavior. Attendance and participation in group should be mandatory at twice a week sessions. Role training may be given in the group. Initially, individual contacts with the Agent center around school, job or family problems.

10. <u>Suggested Techniques for Achieving Goals</u>. Create situation in which Cfc's genuine feelings can be expressed and rewarded, regardless of the content of the feelings. Demonstrate that the Agent is concerned about Cfc by willingness to control his or her behavior (implying that he is worth controlling). Accept Cfc's need for peer support (even if peers are delinquent). By directly meeting some of the Cfc's childlike dependency needs, reduce his reliance on such compensatory mechanisms as denial of needs and rejection of others as potential need-gratifiers. Reduce stereotyping of others via peer group feedback, role playing, by rewarding direct interaction with Agent. Encourage the Cfc to try new activities, reward him for effort and accomplishment. Build self-esteem wherever possible.

11. <u>Kind of Help the Agent Needs</u>. Agent needs community organization knowledge as well as a working knowledge of local subcultures Group treatment training and/or consultation is needed. Agent needs supervisory support 1n sorting out genuine response from "conning," and in helping the Cfc move beyond behavioral change toward attitude and self-definition change.

12. <u>Questions</u>. Is it possible to get beyond behavioral change with all Cfcs? If not, how can crime and delinquency be prevented after Project support is removed?

My Supplemental Description

Though I agree with the above description, I find it difficult to identify with it. I've dealt with the Cfcs primarily in controlled residential settings; however, I've also associated with them and their families in the community. It may be that that relationship causes me to see them in a different light, or perspective. It may simply be that they sense my genuine concern for them. The way they group in both the community and the institution can be intimidating to those not familiar with their ways. If the agent responds with counterintimidating behavior, it can trigger an aggressive response.

I believe that the statements regarding the rejection of adults *("Has given up on satisfying relationships with adults. Perceives adults as being unable or unwilling to meet his dependency needs. Does perceive peers as being able to meet these needs.")* say much about the Cfc. I think this may be indicative of a fear that he is unable to handle difficult situations on his own. In an institutional setting he feels uncomfortable with staff that lack confidence and the ability to maintain order.

At the Preston School we found a dramatic change in the attitude of the Cfcs when we changed our methods from an Authoritarian/

Disciplinarian approach to an insightful therapeutic environment. They changed from aggressive hostility to cooperative support of the staff and program. The Chicano, or Mexican American youths, seemed to benefit most; they were the most organized and regimented of the racial groups.

They developed a trust and loyalty to the regular unit staff. However, on one occasion, a night supervisor who didn't know or understand our wards misinterpreted the activity of one ward, felt threatened, and called for security support. Security forces arrived in a threatening manner and frightened the youths, who in turn became defensive and riotous. A regular staff member was called in for support. On his arrival the wards settled right down and the incident ended. Handled appropriately, the incident would have never occurred. The contrast found in this incident is indicative of the fact that they are reachable by reliable, predictable and caring adults.

I also found that when encouraged to do so, they responded well to activities requiring a concerted cooperative effort. They did well in any activity requiring teamwork.

At O.H. Close School, with a therapeutic environment, racial factors were rarely an issue, our youths associated on the basis of common interests and skills. When talking about the streets they lived on, they gravitated toward those of their race. Intellectual activities were shared with those of common intellects. Athletics were shared with those of common skills, etc.

The environment and the staff attitude enabled them to progressively benefit from insight therapy.

As with all I-3s, they are means oriented rather than goal oriented. Discussions, related to their behavior, is most productive when the means and goals are related. Discussing goals without their relation to the means is counterproductive. In an interview that news commentator Ted Koppel had with a gang following a Los Angeles riot, Koppel insisted on determining the purpose, or the goal, of their riot. They tried to explain to him that that's the way it was done by their rules. Communications were completely blocked because neither Koppel nor the gang understood the other. Without an understanding of how gangs function, you cannot comprehend the motivation behind their behavior.

I've had little experience working with Cfcs as a group in the community. However, I worked with many in controlled residential settings:

1. At Preston, my first assignment was with the "Stone-Out" unit. This unit was comprised of troublemakers from other units, wards that were being shunned (stoned-out) by their peer groups and a high percentage of Cfcs who segregated themselves by race, forming peer groups loyal to their leaders and their members.
2. At O.H. Close during the initial stages of developing a differential treatment plan I was the Senior Youth Counselor of the first living unit, which was comprised of Cfcs.

At the time I began working at Preston School of Industry it was considered the most dangerous CYA facility. They were employing a Disciplinarian/Authoritarian philosophy of treatment believing that discipline was needed to turn these hard-core delinquents into non-delinquents. This was a very hostile environment. As a consequence, the *wards* turned to their peer groups for support, as well as protection. These groups were racially oriented. The institution, in an effort to counter the racial groupings, attempted to force integration, which I believe backfired and only reinforced the need for segregation and increased some hostility toward and distrust of the staff. This merely reinforced the Cfcs distrust of adults.

I wasn't comfortable with the methods being employed, but I assumed the administration was more knowledgeable and experienced than I, so I attempted to learn from this experience. After I had been there for about six months we had a change of administration. This was in the early 1960s, a time when there was much research and experimentation occurring in an effort to find effective treatment strategies. The new superintendent, supported these new concepts. Six living units were chosen to experiment with some of these innovations. The unit I was on was one of these six.

We began by creating caseloads on the living units. Then we gradually improved the recreation programs. We next introduced small group counseling. Here again, it was a gradual process that began with reflective counseling and progressed to directed counseling with some insight therapy. We then introduced community meetings, followed by staff critiques of the meetings, which gradually evolved into the forerunner of treatment teams. As each of these activities was introduced, we found changes in peer relations and relations with staff. The hostile and violent- prone environment progressively diminished to a more amiable environment for both wards and staff.

The Cfcs on my units made dramatic changes in their attitude toward peers of other ethnic groups and staff. At the time I believed that each of the innovations contributed in some way to this development. In reflecting on the progressions of those developments I came to realize that the staff changed their attitudes as well. This wasn't true of all staff or all units, but on the units I was assigned to, this was so. The youths became more cooperative and I became more liberal. These changes were so gradual and subtle that they were hardly discernible.

Except for the initial contacts, I seemed to have little difficulty in developing rapport with the Cfcs. When I would arrive on a new unit there was initial suspicion and testing. This was a ritualistic process, which usually took about two weeks. On the third unit I supervised I short-circuited this process by confronting them with the process and giving them an honest evaluation of my position, attitude and expectations. I believe my open honesty alleviated their fears and suspicions. I gained their respect, and demonstrated that I wasn't a new supervisor, and understood the ways of institutional life.

At O.H. Close we had a totally different environment and set of circumstances. It had a new and unique physical setup, and no prior traditions. The treatment program was based on the model my staff and I had developed at the Fricot Ranch School. We began with a heterogeneous group of twelve wards. The institution wasn't quite ready to begin the treatment process in its entirety, but certain methods were employed. During this initial period, relationships between wards and staff were far more intimate than the initial contacts in other established facilities.

As our numbers grew, the institution was divided into homogeneous groups. This first group was comprised of Cfcs. Through the treatment process, a non-delinquent environment was established. The wards appreciated living in a non-threatening environment. In as much as they were means oriented *("Use of formulas tends to be rigid, indiscriminate, stereotyped and absolutistic. Differential application of rules because of individual differences or because of situational differences is minimal."),* the non-delinquent values established through the treatment process became the applied formulas for functioning.

This contrasted dramatically from that found at Preston earlier. As I said, the Preston unit was comprised of troublemakers from other units, wards that were being shunned (stoned-out) by their peer groups and a high percentage of Cfcs who segregated themselves by race, forming peer groups loyal to their leaders and their members.

Both the Fricot and O.H. Close units used the modified therapeutic community concept, but the Preston unit was still in a developmental stage. Though each of the treatment methods employed contributed to the environmental change on all three units, I believe the community meetings had the greatest impact in uniting the units and giving them a sense of pride and identity with their community.

In the racially oriented units, in prior years, each group oriented new arrivals with the rules of their group. On my units, contrary to many other residential settings, we had no rules posted, nor did we have any specific social rules the wards were to abide by. On the surface, this might give the impression that we had an anarchical community. Such was not the case. On the one hand, as explained in a community meeting, by one of the wards, "We have procedures." We had rigid time structuring, and each ward was expected to participate in each of the various treatment modes. We were also governed by specific security measures.

Two of our treatment goals were to help the wards develop insight and foresight as well as appropriate social behavior. I found, with very few exceptions, all of our wards knew right from wrong. Without a list of dos and don'ts and with minimal staff intervention they found it necessary to evaluate their own behavior. In addition, due to the various counseling modes, they found themselves accountable to the other wards on the unit. One point in the program was that the wards were expected to help one another. Destructive criticism was tabooed. (As stated in one community meeting, "If you can't say somethin' good, don't say nothin.") The seeming anarchical structure didn't exist. The wards worked together for their own benefit, and the benefit of each other.

The wards in our program, had an opportunity to make poor choices. These poor choices gave staff and other wards the opportunity to counsel those wards. In many cases, the counseling of ward to ward was more effective than staff to ward.

In the O.H. Close program a self-appointed group would orient new arrivals on the unit values, or the rules that had been established by consensus at the community meetings. The Cfcs, like all I-3s, need structuring. By establishing non-delinquent values through the use of each of our counseling modes, delinquency on the living unit was discouraged by both wards and staff alike.

Here again, as mentioned earlier, relationship building also played a very important part in creating the social climate we achieved. As the description of the Cfc states, he has *given up on satisfying relationships with adults. Perceives adults as being unable or unwilling. to meet his dependency needs. Does perceive peers as being able to meet these needs.* Our program enabled the wards to develop trusting relationships with adults and support from their peers.

Relationship Building with the Cfc

Relationship building with the Cfc is primarily dependent on the attitude, reliability, and genuine concern of the agent.

Initially the agent will be met with caution, suspicion and sometimes hostility. *(Has given up on satisfying relationships with adults. Perceives adults as being unable or unwilling. to meet his dependency needs. Does perceive peers as being able to meet these needs.)* This can change dramatically in a relatively short time, but here again it is dependent on the attitude of the agent. It is dependent on the agent's own behavior; his reliability, dependability, and genuine concern.

The characteristics of the appropriate agent are clearly outlined in the treatment plan:

> *Agent should have the ability to empathize on the*
> *basis of nonverbal modes of communication and*
> *to utilize nonverbal modes in conveying empathy,*
> *and the ability to be aware of primitive drives and*

*defenses against these. Agent should have the ability
to exert friendly but firm parental control, ability to
act promptly and appropriately in order to provide
controls, ability to make definitive decisions and to
act upon them. Agent should be able to understand
the dependency needs underlying the "distance"
facade. He should be able to accept and like the Cfc
while he disapproves (and is willing to punish for)
the misbehavior. When the Cfc "hears" the Agent's
message of concern and comes to the Agent, wanting
to relate as child to parent, the Agent must be
emotionally available.*

As the relationship builds, they can respond to insightful discussions. It also helps if the agent is "streetwise"; communication can be difficult otherwise. Being able to "rap" with a Cfc is a big help in developing relationships. Though the agent must be firm in dealing with misbehavior he must be fair and just.

One of the primary difficulties the agent encounters in communicating with the Cfc is the realization that the Cfc is means oriented. The rules of the Cfc's group take precedence over any rational goal. The interview that Ted Koppel had with one of the gangs in Los Angeles was confusing to both the gang leaders and to Koppel, because Koppel was speaking to them in terms of "goals" and they replied in terms of "means." There was a total failure of meaningful communication. Neither could comprehend the position of the other.

After the agent has established a comfortable and trusted relationship with the Cfc he can discuss goals, but in relationship to the means. Cfc's can be quite cooperative with trusted adults.

An example of this occurred while working on the stone-out unit at Preston.

I had a long standing relationship with the leader of the chicanos. It began when we were both new at Preston. At the time wards were discouraged from close relationships with staff. Somehow we had developed an affinity for each other through non-verbal communication. I was only on his unit for a short time during my training and we had virtually no direct contact. As time passed, though, we had minor contacts from time to time, but only had the opportunity for momentary non-verbal recognition of each other. In the many months that followed he became the leader of the chicanos and I had developed a reputation with many of the wards. Most wards saw me as one who sincerely cared and someone they could discuss their concerns with.

Being the leader of the chicanos he was seen as a "troublemaker" on the units he had been assigned to. Because of this he was transferred to the unit where I was working. It was then that we finally had a chance to talk together. Between our past encounters and my reputation he felt free to talk with me. On one occasion, I'm not sure what prompted the conversation, but we were discussing the stone-outs. Understanding their need to follow the rules of their group, I pointed out a flaw in their rules. Their intent was to punish the stone-outs, but it didn't seem to be working as they intended. The stone-outs were going home much sooner than the group members. The group members saw extended periods of incarceration as macho. I pointed out that though they intended to punish the stone-outs, they were really doing the stone-outs a favor; they were doing less time. I then pointed out that if they work together to help each other get released, they might achieve their intent. The stone-outs would end up doing more time and the members would be going home sooner.

In effect, I was suggesting that changing the rules might benefit the members more. In this case, I was speaking in terms of the group's rules and the benefits to the group. I was accepting the group and their rules rather than attacking them. I don't know how much affect this had on the chicanos, but they seemed to become less hostile and more cooperative. However, at the same time we had changed to a more therapeutic environment, which also influenced the relationships between wards and staff.

On another occasion, when the racial barriers were still in the process of dissolving, but not completely resolved, I noticed that all the blacks and all the chicanos were lined up with their respective groups. This hadn't occurred for quite a while. The tension was apparent and it appeared that we were about to have a racial melee.

I gathered the Chicanos together in a separate room. I asked them, "What's up?" In the past I wasn't likely to get an answer. But at this point my relationship was such that they trusted me enough to reveal that someone had told them that the blacks were going to jump them.

I asked them if they were looking for a hassle. They said no. They didn't want trouble.

After I found out who told them, I asked them to play it "cool" and give me a chance to handle it. They promised they would.

I then gathered the blacks and repeated the same questions with them. They revealed the same thing that the chicanos had. They also said they didn't want any trouble either. They also revealed the name of the person who told them the chicanos were going to jump them.

It seemed we had an agitator on the unit. I told the blacks to play it cool too, because the chicanos weren't looking for trouble either.

I called the leaders of the chicanos and the blacks and told them what happened. I also told them to leave the agitator to me, that I would take care of him. And everything was cool; nobody wanted trouble. They returned to their groups and told them what I had said, the tensions disappeared and the groups were integrated again.

I was able to resolve the problem not necessarily by my method, but through my relationship with the wards. They knew I was concerned about them, that I could be trusted and relied on, so they gave me the opportunity to do what I did.

Though, as I mentioned earlier, I've had little experience in working with Cfcs in the community, I've had considerable experience in working with them in a controlled residential setting. I believe the key to treating them is the relationship of the agent. With an established relationship they seem capable of responding well to counseling and insight therapy. With an ongoing, reliable, relationship they can turn from dependence on their peers and ultimately trust the adult agent. Evidence to support this was indicated by the low recidivism rate of the Cfcs. The Cfcs of O.H. Close had one of the lowest recidivism rates in the state.

CHAPTER 4

The I-3 Cfm

From the 1965 edition, here are the characteristics of the Cfm:

Ways of Perceiving the World:

1. <u>Self Perception as Inferior to Others.</u> No felt capacity to be responsible for control of self and environment. Has a childlike stance. In comparison with others (rather than with a self ideal) he typically considers himself less adequate. Self-perception as "low man on the totem pole". Denies leadership interest. Presents himself as dependent on the rules of others for keeping him out of trouble.

2. <u>Self Description in Conventional and Socially Desirable Terms</u>. Initially describes himself as "average", "normal". Presents himself as sincere, cooperative, well-intentioned, easy to get along with. He may also give a picture of himself quite at odds with this description, especially when interviewed with regard to specific behavioral incidents.

3. <u>Anti-Social Behavior Ego-Alien</u>. With rare exceptions, he is uncomfortable with "delinquent" label. Delinquency as a way of life is not congruent with self-image. Typically feels that he became involved in the delinquent act as a result of external forces.

4. <u>Overestimates the Power of Others</u>. Is especially sensitive to the needs of others to control him. Sees control or "giving" figures as having expectations of him to conform to their standards, and assumes the power of others to be overwhelming when he does not meet these expectations. He overestimates the likelihood of the use and the forcefulness of the power.

5. <u>Absence of Sense of Belonging, Including to Delinquent Subculture</u>. Since his response is to immediate power structure, his actions tend to be somewhat unpredictable to delinquent peers, so that he is not a completely acceptable member of the group. In an interview, he may at first maintain his full group membership, but later admit his marginal membership - typically by suggesting that "the group isn't all that important to him".

6. <u>Non-Rejection of Adults</u>. Has not given up completely on establishing satisfying relationships with adults even though he is somewhat pessimistic and typically anticipates rejection (though may deny this). Relative "openness" and trust, compared to other I-3 subtypes. Likes adults who are "helpful", or "understanding", who take time to "explain things", who "correct" him, who (as a sign of interest) "correct" him, who recognize that he "wants to do right".

7. <u>Self Concept as a "Generator" of Response in Others</u>. Attempts to handle situations with a formula (surface conformity), trying to bring about desired outcomes. Typically (and consciously) feels he has to actively "turn off" the threatening or overwhelming aspects of the world and to "turn on" at a minimum the neutral, non-threatening aspects and preferably the supportive, giving aspects.

8. <u>Nature of Crises</u>. Anxiety arises when (a) he is rejected by significant adult or peer group; or when (b) he becomes aware of "demand" from others which he feels unable to meet (for example, may be caught in middle of opposing demands - adults vs. peers - or may be faced with unclear or ambiguous standards for meeting demands).

Ways of Responding to the World:

9. <u>Rigid Application of Formulas</u>. Use of formulas tends to be indiscriminate, stereotyped, inflexible and absolutistic. Differential application of rules because of individual differences among others or because of situational differences is minimal. Major formulas involve (a) his buying support through immediate conformity to the actual or perceived demands of others, or (b) when formula (a) is not perceived as succeeding his forcing others to reject him via his misbehavior.

10. <u>Situation-Bound in the Extreme</u>. Has difficulty in holding in consciousness any information beyond that represented by and relevant to immediate stimuli (perceived as pressure). Little capacity to delay response to immediate stimuli.

11. <u>Need for Social Approval</u>. Completely dominated by this need. Will say or do anything in order not to be disapproved of by those immediately surrounding him. Yields to peer group pressure in the presence of peers and to adult pressure in the presence of adults. Over compliant in an interview, responding primarily with assumed socially desirable answer. Major focus of social interactions is to avoid pain or punishment and/or to seek approval for his behavior.

12. <u>Self Presentation as Passive</u>. Presents self to adults as relatively passive. Appears fearful of assertiveness. Feelings of resentment are present but expression is usually suppressed. May complain about others not behaving according to his expectations; this is done in a direct confrontive manner only if he has given up on the relationship with a particular adult.

13. <u>Pattern of Flight</u>. Major methods of handling crises are those of psychological withdrawal or actual flight (runaway). Withdraws to avoid doing something which he believes will or may lead to his being rejected or disapproved of by others, or lead to his having support withdrawn by others.

14. <u>Relationships with Adults</u>. Commonly presents self as "helpless"; "pulls" for protection. Often appears openly fearful and anticipates his being rejected. Is able to develop strong dependency relationship with sympathetic adult.

15. <u>Relationships with Peers</u>. Does not have "close" relationships (e.g., emotionally intimate and/or sharing of highly personalized experiences and feelings) with peers. Important to him to have companions but, as

with adults, fearful of rejection. Peers tend not to trust him.

16. <u>Reasons for Delinquency</u>. Offense behavior as one or more of the following meanings: Attempt to gain peer approval, fear of and/or flight from disappointing, emotionally non-supportive, indifferent or rejecting parental or other adult figures.

17. <u>Attitude Towards Delinquency</u>. In the presence of peers, may show eagerness to commit delinquent acts but evidences no strong loyalty and commitment to a delinquent code apart from its capacity to meet or not meet his needs for immediate approval from individual members of a group. Cannot say "no" to demands or suggestions for deviancy. Is fearful of being called "chicken", "coward", and "sissy". Is able to recognize retrospectively that what he did was a mistake, but at the time of offense is not able to disengage himself from the demands of the moment. Upon apprehension, may make some effort to manipulate himself out of consequences. May claim he has "learned his lesson"; may say he will now "stay away from the boys who got him into trouble". When unable to avoid the consequences, he may become sullen, resentful, and pouty. Does not attribute maliciousness or malevolence to his behavior.

18. <u>Acceptance of Emotionality</u>. Compared with other I-3 subtypes, open acceptance of feeling response in himself. May admit to emotions (anger, sadness, fear) in interview situation (may cry openly) but tends to minimize the influence of these emotions on his behavior (delinquent or otherwise).

My Supplemental Description

Of all the I-3s, the Cfms have the lowest self-esteem yet have a greater potential than the others. They give the initial impression that they are weak dependents. They are frequently scapegoated, used and abused. They have an affinity for Mps that confuse many caseworkers. Mps systematically destroy what little self-esteem the Cfms have and drive them into a deeper withdrawal. They are the most common victims of child or spousal abuse, both physically and psychologically. They most often marry Mps and in turn propagate Mps, Cfms, and/or I-2s. The Mp children in turn abuse the Cfm parent.

In the description above it states: *"Major focus of social interactions is to avoid pain or punishment and/or to seek approval for his behavior."* On the surface this appears to be so, but in reality and the point that confuses caseworkers is they repeatedly return to abusive spouses. It's as though they have some masochistic tendencies.

For the record, let's revisit the description of the Cfm's attitude towards delinquency:

> *In the presence of peers, may show eagerness to commit delinquent acts but evidences no strong loyalty and commitment to a delinquent code apart from its capacity to meet or not meet his needs for immediate approval from individual members of a group. Cannot say "no" to demands or suggestions for deviancy. Is fearful of being called "chicken", "coward", and "sissy". Is able to recognize retrospectively that what he did was a mistake, but at the time of offense is not able to disengage himself from the demands of the moment. Upon apprehension, may make some effort to manipulate himself out of consequences. May claim he has*

"learned his lesson"; may say he will now "stay away from the boys who got him into trouble". When unable to avoid the consequences, he may become sullen, resentful, and pouty. Does not attribute maliciousness or malevolence to his behavior.

Here again, he is most likely attracted to an Mp, who encourages a delinquent behavior, not for support but the ultimate degradation of the Cfm. It also states that he can not say "no" to demands or suggestions for deviancy. Due to his immaturity and limited insight and foresight he is highly vulnerable to suggestion with the thought that this will make him acceptable. This ultimately leads to consequences and the ambiguity in his understanding of what has occurred; the behavior was not intended for maliciousness, but for social acceptance.

Another dilemma the Cfm finds himself in is that once he's been controlled by an Mp he is highly vulnerable to the same treatment from other Mps. The Mp has such a rigid formula for operating and where all Mps have virtually identical behavior patterns, the Cfm is conditioned by one Mp and another Mp merely picks up where the previous one left off. Thus the Cfm is caught up in a self-perpetuating conditioned behavior pattern that he neither understands nor knows how to defend against. This adds to the Cfm's feelings of helplessness and the urge to withdraw into himself.

Let's revisit Points #8 and #12 respectively:

Anxiety arises when (a) he is rejected by significant adult or peer group; or when (b) he becomes aware of "demand" from others which he feels unable to meet (for example, may be caught in middle of opposing demands - adults vs. peers - or may be faced with unclear or ambiguous standards for meeting demands).

When faced with opposing demands, he most frequently responds to what appears to him as the strongest force. This will be explained in more detail in the treatment strategy for the Cfm.

> *Presents self to adults as relatively passive. Appears fearful of assertiveness. Feelings of resentment are present but expression is usually suppressed. May complain about others not behaving according to his expectations; this is done in a direct confrontive manner only if he has given up on the relationship with a particular adult."* This can be broadened and be more specific in identifying the Cfm. They are especially sensitive to criticism. They either rationalize to justify their behavior, or counter attack with criticism of the perceived attacker. At other times they will merely withdraw suppressing their anger, or simply, openly cry. Though they strongly object to being criticized themselves, they are unusually critical of those who don't meet their expectations without any perception of the differences in their attitude and that of others.

They seem to have an internal conflict between their self-esteem and their actual potential. Though they strive for social acceptance, they defeat themselves and set themselves up for rejection because they seem unable to perceive what will really please others. At the same time their perception can be very keen in modeling themselves after others, or learning through observation.

As for their immaturity, they enjoy child type games, like those enjoyed by preadolescents— simple games with few complexities.

When appropriately treated they seem more responsive than other I-3s and seem better able to improve their ability to function in society. I've seen dramatic changes, many times, in my work with Cfms.

Treatment Plan for I-3 CFM:
(1966 Revision)

1. <u>Goals</u>. Develop image of Treatment Agent as giving, caring, non-threatening in order to help Cfm feel valued as a person and feel a sense of belonging; increase recognition of and differentiation among his or her feelings; help Cfm accept the legitimacy of his feelings; increase awareness of his impact on others and their impact on him; change self-definition in direction of security in decision-making, ability to meet demands of others, ability to assert himself with others, capacity for growth, personal worth, "good person;" encourage identification with adequate adult (Agent, Foster Parent).

2. <u>Placement Plan</u>. Place in own home initially unless Cfm requests removal. Temporary foster home frequently required, especially with younger Cfm's. Foster home should be capable of dealing with negative behavior, and accepting and supportive of Cfm in spite of any negative behavior on his or her part. Foster mother should be able to accept open expressions of dependent feelings. Foster father should be comfortable in husband and father roles, able to give and control, able to accept Cfm's clinging to foster mother. There should be no other children in the home (first choice) or the children should be younger.

3. <u>Family Variables</u>. Relevant change in natural family difficult to bring about. Help family or foster family to provide consistent, non-threatening structure. Increase understanding of Cfm by interpreting his behavior to

family. Attempt to protect Cfm from emotional damage by parent(s). Formal family group therapy (conjoint family therapy) appears to be inappropriate.

4. <u>Location of Community Supports</u>. Make use of neighborhood recreation programs if they exist and if any support and protection for Cfm is available there. Agent should search out and encourage outside relationships with supportive adults so that long-term over dependence on the Agent is avoided.

5. <u>School Recommendations</u>. Problem lies with impossibility of teacher giving Cfm enough individual attention and support to meet his or her needs. Conferences with teachers, interpreting Cfm's problems and suggesting techniques for handling, may help Cfm survive in the school system for a time. Program should offer tutoring and remedial work.

6. <u>Job recommendations</u>. Cfm fearful and passive re job hunting and keeping. Role-playing employment situation helps him or her prepare. Neighborhood Youth Corps employment training programs are useful when situations are not too interpersonally demanding.

7. <u>Peer Group and Recreation Variables</u>. Natural peer group relationships are superficial and transitory. Develop a homogeneous (i.e., all Cfms) project peer group, which offers acceptance and belonging. (Heterogeneous groups are overwhelming initially and Cfm assumes lowest status role.) Increase Cfm's understanding of peers so that he or she can better predict and relate to others. Encourage Cfm to utilize Treatment Center activity facilities, gradually increasing his ability to interact with non-Cfms. When he is ready, help Cfm move out into non-project activities.

8. <u>Kind of Controls</u>. Consistency and non-threat essential. Provide a structure of clarity, concreteness and understandability. Agent should present behavioral standards ("I want you to go to school.") but not necessarily punish if standards are violated. Detention may be defeating of overall goals. If detention is necessary in order to maintain Cfm in program, Agent should communicate "concern," not threat. "Chewing out" techniques are appropriate after relationship with Agent has been established. Encourage foster parents to provide controls and suggest techniques.

9. <u>Agent Characteristics</u>. Agent should have the ability to empathize on the basis of nonverbal modes of communication and to utilize nonverbal modes in conveying empathy, the ability to be aware of primitive drives and defenses against these. Agent should be optimistic, patient, generous, self-reliant, and spontaneous. He or she should have confidence in "being himself," have basic trust and receive pleasure from giving. Agent must be tolerant of expressions of dependence and be able to reflect a parental stance of love plus strength. He must also be accepting of growth in the Cfm. Additionally, he or she should be seen by the Cfm as an enabler, a "ways and means" person, who can teach the Cfm the ways to adulthood,

10. <u>Treatment Methods</u>. Individual contact between Agent and Cfm - as much as possible - emphasizing on-the-spot treatment (significant interaction). Cfm group meetings twice a week - group resembling family group with agent in parent role and group members as siblings. Meetings should be focused on significant interactions (discussion-focused when possible in terms of Cfms' tolerance), with emphasis on current interpersonal

dealings and techniques for staying out of trouble rather than on past history and reasons (dynamics) for behavior. Cfm activity group to create feelings of support and belonging. Teach methods of becoming an adult (independent) via role-playing techniques.

11. <u>Suggested Techniques for Achieving Treatment Goals</u>. Demonstrate support and concern for Cfm while minimizing threat of adult's power. Search out Cfm's negative expectations of and negative reactions to Agent and accept these negative feelings without rejection of Cfm. Communicate through actions as well as words. Give material things (food, clothing); give time and attention in activities with him or her. Label feelings as they occur. Reward participation and intention rather than level of performance or end product. Encourage Cfm to make decisions and to choose among alternatives. Reassure regarding ability to make decisions and point out when Cfm has taken action on his own. Increase Cfm's awareness of others' impact on him (including family, foster family, school, peer group) and his impact on them by explaining and interpreting. "Nurture" without making decisions for Cfm. Support Cfm's efforts to plan for himself.

12. Kind of Help the Agent Needs. Casework supervision to support Agent's time investment and commitment; consultation regarding conceptualization of dynamics as the Cfm grows and changes in treatment; support in using this plan with Cfms from Agents using other plans to handle other sub-types; help from peers and supervisor in order to avoid over-identification with Cfm or prolongation of the Cfm's dependence; support in keeping the caseload of Cfms low so that sufficient time will be available for treatment activities; Treatment Center which is constantly available to Cfms

for activities; transportation for Cfms to the Center; adequate budget for food, clothing.

13. <u>Questions.</u> Should Agent aim for higher maturity level (I-4) in treatment with Cfm or instead for a more acceptable adjustment at the I-3 level? Is it possible to tell at intake which path is more appropriate with a particular Cfm? If a Cfm is moving toward an I-4, level, is psychotherapy appropriate?

Strategy

The Cfm has an extremely low self-esteem. This of course is true of all I-3s. The difference between the Cfm and other I-3s is in the way he presents himself: he typically considers himself less adequate and perceives himself as the low man on the totem pole. Furthermore, as described, *he presents self to adults as relatively passive. Appears fearful of assertiveness. Feelings of resentment are present but expression is usually suppressed. May complain about others not behaving according to his expectations; this is done in a direct confrontive manner...*

The Cfm overestimates the power of others and as stated, is especially sensitive to the needs of others to control him, seeing *control or "giving" figures as having expectations of him to conform to their standards, and assumes the power of others to be overwhelming when he does not meet these expectations. He overestimates the likelihood of the use and the forcefulness of the power.*

He is also completely dominated by the need for social approval. The Cfm *will say or do anything in order not to be disapproved of by those immediately surrounding him. Yields to peer group pressure in the presence of peers and to adult pressure in the presence of adults. Over compliant in an interview, responding primarily with assumed socially desirable answer. Major focus of social interactions is to avoid pain or punishment and/or to seek approval for his behavior.*

These characteristics I believe are, for the most part, environmentally determined. They are, the progeny of Mps most often coupled with a Cfm, biological parent. Raised in this environment they are abused, used and frequently rejected by the Mp and shown how to respond by the Cfm parent.

Considering the irrational behavior of Mps, their fear of intimacy and their bullying attitude toward those weaker than themselves, the Cfm is a victim of the insensitive Mp. Mps are relentless in their efforts to destroy people. They drive the Cfm into a hole of withdrawal where passivity becomes a defense against the assaults.

I've found, in working with Cfms, raising their self-esteem is a key factor in helping Cfms become more assertive, and thus more functional. This can be achieved in many ways.

One of the most prevalent ways is for the agent to present himself as a nurturing, supportive adult whose concern is comparable to that of a parent. His initial treatment is most effective when treated similarly as an I-2 with much recognition, praise and encouragement. However, unlike an I-2, the Cfm has more insight and is more vulnerable or amenable to suggestion. *(Yields to peer group pressure in the presence of peers and to adult pressure in the presence of adults.)*

In my early work with Cfms I took advantage of their submission to pressure. Our programs required that the wards participate in one-on-one counseling, small group counseling, and community meetings. Forcefully demanding his participation created a crisis. (See Point #8, Nature of Crises.) However, once they began speaking, in each of the counseling situations, they gained recognition, support and encouragement from both staff and wards alike. As they increased their participation, their self-esteem improved as well as their relations with peers and staff.

This method seemed to cause an excessive amount of anxiety. I later tried autosuggestion and found it to be far more successful and less stressful. I used this method in both residential settings and in the field. Where contacts occurred on a regular schedule, I had them tell me something good about themselves every time we met. At first they didn't have any idea what I was talking about. They could think of nothing good about themselves. Initially, I would have to prompt them and point out some of their merits. I would then instruct them that each time I saw them I expected them to tell me something good about themselves. I told them I didn't care what they said, and even permitted them to repeat the same qualities. It wasn't long before they would anticipate my contact and would practice in their internal dialogues, what they would tell me.

This process increased their awareness of the many qualities that they really had. Soon they were more verbal and more actively participating in achieving their goals. Initially, some would merely mumble their responses. On the advice of Dr. Robert Goulding, my TA mentor, I required that they speak up loud and clear. As they did this their confidence increased. Occasionally I would encounter a Cfm, who in my initial interview would merely respond by shaking his head. When this happened, I countered this by turning my back on them so that they had to respond verbally.

In each case where the Cfm's self-esteem improved dramatically, his characteristics also changed within its current environment. They became more assertive, more verbal, and increased their identity, feeling a part of the groups they were associated with. In some cases, they were no longer treated as scapegoats, but on the contrary, became leaders on their units. I believe their influence varied according to their intellect.

The CTP staff raised questions about what could be expected of a Cfm: *Should Agent aim for higher maturity level (I-4) in treatment with Cfm or instead for a more acceptable adjustment at the I-3 level? Is it possible to tell at intake which path is more appropriate with a particular Cfm? If a Cfm is moving toward an I-4, level, is psychotherapy appropriate?*

In my opinion, I don't believe the Cfm can reach the maturity level of an I-4. Though he may change dramatically as an I-3 Cfm, he still has limited insight and foresight. This is a major difference between an I-3 and an I-4.

The Cfm must be protected from and disassociate himself with Mps. The Cfm is most often raised by an Mp parent and has Mp siblings. Cfms and Mps have an affinity for one another. The Mp needs to control and thus victimizes the passive Cfm. The Cfm is conditioned by the Mp at an early stage in life to respond to specific cues. Where the Mp has such a rigid behavior pattern and where Mps have virtually identical behavior patterns, in their relationships with Cfms, the conditioning process continues from one Mp to another—one picks up where the other leaves off. I've invariably seen Cfms, who are functioning well, come in contact with an Mp and suddenly revert back to a previous behavior.

The Cfm has a limited ability to internalize what he learns. He is best treated with behavior modification using operant and respondent conditioning reinforced with sensory stimulation; generalized reinforcers. Proximity plays an important role in the effects and sustenance of the conditioned responses. Of the many Cfms I've worked with, those that are able to recognize the behavior patterns of the Mps still have difficulty understanding ways to counter the Mp stimuli. Mps use key phrases, and masterfully applied nonverbal cues to frustrate and confuse the Cfm.

In the marriage counseling of a Cfm and an Mp, I found it necessary to have the Cfm turn his back to the Mp and firmly instruct the Mp to "shut up" in order to free the Cfm to explain his position. The Cfm was instructed to do the same thing when they were confronted by some judiciary authority. Not doing this, the results would make the Cfm appear to be the bad guy and the Mp the good guy. On the other hand, when the Cfm followed the instructions the truth was exposed, not only by the testimony of the Cfm, but the Mps' loss of control, which caused him to show his true character thus exonerating the Cfm.

The success or failure of a Cfm is primarily dependent upon those he associates with and his specific intellect. Those I've observed who are relatively successful in their professions and relatively successful in their relationships still maintain their core personalities and basic behavior patterns. Their behavior may become more sophisticated, but their motivation remains the same. Their need for social acceptance continues to dominate their behavior. When in the presence of an Mp, they can be observed to change directions based on the suggestions of the Mp. When in a heterogeneous group, careful observation can detect the anxiety of the Cfm, who strives to balance his stance to accommodate both the Mps and the I-4s when a controversy arises. He does a balancing act, trying to agree with both sides. The controversy is provoked by an Mp attempting to hook someone into an argument. Those of a higher maturity level will either find themselves caught in a meaningless argument or, in most cases, will not take the bait and ignore or minimize the Mps statement. This is often dependent upon the makeup of the group by I Level types, and the numbers of each. The Mp is reluctant to provoke an argument when outnumbered by those of a higher maturity level.

In conclusion, though the Cfm may be quite successful, and a leader in his profession, his core personality and basic behavior patterns remain constant. Here again, it must be emphasized that the I Level descriptions describe each of the personality types *"...not at the level which reflects their maximum capabilities under conditions of extreme comfort, but rather are categorized at that level which represents their typical level, of functioning or, their capacity to function, under conditions of stress."* When things are going their way they can function quite well; but when under stress, what they perceive as stress, the I Level description becomes quite apparent.

Recognizing their I Level enables the agent to predict their behavior and recognize their needs. Though the Cfm has limited insight, they seem to have more insight than any of the other I-3s and by comparison are much easier to work with. As their self-esteem improves, they are far less dependent. As they become more verbal, their logic and reasoning becomes more apparent as well as their insight and foresight.

Let's turn to the topic of employment and job recommendations. The Cfm is described as being fearful and passive about job hunting and job keeping.

One of my field assignments was to work with a family with several children. This also included working with the father, who was a Cfm. My focus was the children, but in my discussions with the father regarding the children I recognized he had needs, too. He was unemployed but felt he should work to help support the family. In discussing employment with him, he stated that he was really needed at home for the sake of the children, as well as other superfluous reasons. Still, he felt he should be employed.

So we checked on the Internet to see what was available that he might be able to handle. He found several jobs, but didn't follow up with an application. Finally, he revealed that he really wanted to drive a semi truck. It had been a childhood dream. He also had an extensive collection of model trucks of all different dimensions. I suggested that he look into acquiring a truck driving position. He needed training, but the agency agreed to assist him in paying for the necessary training. In the course of our conversations, he stated what he had to do to get the training and a position he wanted. I suggested that he do what was necessary. He said he would do that. I felt he was trying to set up another avoidance situation. I confronted him with the question "When?" I forced a commitment. He answered, "Tomorrow."

Reaching this point had taken a few months. In our earlier conversations I recognized a very low self-esteem. In recognition of this I began autosuggestion treatment by having him tell me something good about himself at each of my appointments. Raising his self-esteem gave him the strength to follow up on his commitment. Without digressing too much, I'd like to mention that he now drives a semi truck. While he didn't pass his first driving test due to a minor error, he went back and successfully passed the test. This is an example of a much improved Cfm with more assertiveness and a much improved self-confidence.

For some reason that I can't accurately identify, Cfms seemed to have an affinity for me. Though one unit I worked on was primarily for Mps, occasionally we would have a Cfm placed on our unit. The social worker who assigned wards to the various caseloads, no matter how large my caseload was, would always assign them to me because as he said, no matter whose caseload he assigned them to, they would always gravitate to me.

One Cfm assigned to me had one of the lowest, if not the lowest self-esteems I had ever encountered. When he first arrived on the unit the Mps tried to scapegoat him. When he was assigned to my caseload he started following me around like a little puppy dog. He was right behind me from the minute I arrived until I went home. He never said anything, just followed close behind. I got the impression, as most people do with Cfms, that he was helpless and dim- witted.

All incoming and outgoing mail had to be censored by the wards caseworker. After this ward had been on the unit for a couple of weeks, he handed me a letter to be censored. When I read the letter I was amazed at what a beautiful letter it was. Usually most of he mail was very simple, a couple of sentences and requests for goodies. This letter was such a contrast to the impression I had of this youth that I asked him, "Who wrote this for you?" He told me he did. I was amazed and praised him for such a beautiful letter.

Later that day I spoke to his school teachers to find out how well he was doing in school. They reported that he was doing well and was a pretty smart youth. I decided to use autosuggestion to raise his self-esteem. As this method progressed, he began to speak up in our small group meetings, and gradually in our community meetings.

Within six months he became a leader on the unit. When he spoke up at community meetings the rest of the wards listened.

During this same period I went on vacation for two weeks. While I was gone, the youths of my caseload insisted on continuing their small group meetings. One of the youths in my group was there on a long-term commitment. He became so well versed in transactional analysis that I had begun using him as a co-therapist. The youth I was discussing and this youth felt they could conduct a small group meeting as co-therapists. Both were identifying with me at this time. They requested of the supervising staff to hold a meeting without a staff member's presence. n as much as the counseling office was a glassed enclosure, the staff agreed. On my return, the staff reported to me that they had observed the group through the windows and that the group appeared to be well organized and appeared productive.

A month or so later, after this youth had been in the program for about seven months, he was given a furlough in preparation for his release. It seems his visit went well and he was on the bus preparing to return to the institution when he thought to himself, "I'm too important to go back to the institution!" He got off the bus and made the rounds of his hometown. He was located a couple of days later and returned to the institution. When he told me his story, I explained to him that important people are responsible and fulfill their commitments. That although it was true that he was important, he had a responsibility to fulfill his commitment to the CYA.

His treatment goal was to improve his self-esteem and become more active on the unit. This he had done. When I reported this to the parole board and described my response, they didn't add any time to his commitment for "running away" but instead retained his release date.

In both the cases mentioned and with the many other Cfms I've treated, I found that they respond well to respondent and operant conditioning. Using successive approximations reinforced with generalized reinforces such as compliments and encouragement. Raising their self-esteem with autosuggestion and generalized counseling increases their assertiveness and self-confidence. I don't believe psychotherapy is a preferred choice for treatment.

In the two cases cited, both achieved their goals. One had been involved in small group counseling, the other just one-on-one general counseling. One was treated in the field while the other in a controlled residential setting. I believe the one that experienced the institutional basic plan may have gained more self-confidence and assertiveness as a result of participating in one-on-one, small group, and community meetings. I think he simply had more opportunities for meaningful learning experiences that reinforced his behavior.

In both cases as in others, all were treated with warm, friendly, supportive and patient care.

CHAPTER 5

The I-3 Mp

I-3 Mp Characteristics
(1965 Revision)

Ways of Perceiving the World:

1. <u>Satisfied with Mode of Living - Resists Change</u>. Tries
    to give overall impression of feeling that his way of life
    is comfortable, effective and satisfactory. Rejects the
    idea of change in himself, his attitudes, and situations.
    Problems, if admitted, are minimized and are not
    internal struggles, but rather represent conflicts between
    himself and some aspect of the external world (school,
    for example). His "mistakes" (problems with the law)
    are in the past.

2. <u>Self Concept as a "Generator" of Response in Others</u>.
    Overestimates the potential of his formula (conning ,and
    conforming) as a means of being able to control others
    and bring about the desired outcome in any situation.
    If his formula doesn't appear to be working, he does not

perceive the <u>formula </u>is at fault; rather, something went wrong in the application of the formula. Feels he has to "do something to turn the world on". Believes that others will not meet his needs unless he "takes it (the need satisfier) away" from them.

3. <u>Anti-social Behavior not Ego-Alien</u>. Anti-social behavior seen simply as meeting one's own needs, or dealing out to others what they deserve, being smart enough to outsmart others. These acts are an acceptable part of the self-image, and may be defended against criticism so that behavior appears warranted, reasonable and justified.

4. <u>Nature of Crisis</u>. Crisis a result of his application of formula for operating failing to work or a result of perceived threat to his ability to remain in control (of self, others, situations).

5. <u>Pessimism re: Others</u>. Perceives others as being unwilling to meet his dependency needs. Assumes that others will try to "use" him to their own advantage.

6. <u>Others in Terms of His Own Needs and Feelings</u>. His perceptions of others' motivations is similar to that which he sees in himself. No awareness that individual needs and feelings different from his own exist. For example, really believes that everyone operates so as to make a sucker out of the other person before he is made a sucker himself.

7. <u>"Means" Oriented</u>. Characteristically focuses on "means" rather than goals in his interpersonal relationships. Attends primarily to the manipulative operations involved in dealing with others and gets his major

rewards (and his sense of self) from his manipulations. Gets carried away with the scheming and loses sight of the original goal.

8. <u>Does not Appear to Learn from Experience</u>. Functions socially from a rigidly closed frame of reference that is self-reinforcing and consistently rejecting of information that might modify its structure. Selectively attends to, and assimilates, only that part of experience that is congruent with his mode of perceiving, and either fails to perceive or defends against that which is incongruent. Seeks to correct recognized deficiencies and to refine his mode of relating (conning, - conforming, and intimidating), but does not question his perceptual stance regarding the world.

9. <u>Self Perception</u>. May see self in some of the following ways: cynical, "cool", smooth, delinquent, powerful, invulnerable, imperturbable.

Ways of Responding to the World:

10. <u>Rigid Application of Formulas</u>. Use of formulas tends to be rigid, indiscriminate, stereotyped and absolutistic. Differential application of rules because of individual differences or because of situational differences is minimal. Does not manipulate or "con as one of a variety of alternative techniques (as with higher maturity individuals); rather, it is his <u>only</u> formula for operating.

11. <u>Counteractive to Power</u>. Sets up a battleground re: power and control whenever he perceives the power of another as likely to have an impact on him. Fights back against power both subtly and obviously. Active attempts to eliminate restrictions on his freedom. Important to his

self image to be seen as in control of himself and having power over others.

12. <u>Emotionally Insulated</u>. Does not accept the utility of feelings and values as a basis of human relationships. Attempts to create an image of emotional indifference, imperturbability and invulnerability. He denies that he may have strong feelings, that others might elicit these kinds of response, or that such feelings might control his behavior. Will not allow himself to consummate (or is fearful of consummating) relationships in which he is in any way dependent upon another person. Denies and rejects dependency needs as part of himself.

13. <u>Relationships with Others Superficial and Short-Lived</u>. Manages to alienate both authority figures and peer group members after relatively short contact. May originally make quite a positive impression if he so desires. However, continual use of others as objects to gain his own ends, frequently combined interpersonal destructiveness, builds hostility toward him.

14. <u>Reasons for Delinquency</u>. Offense behavior has one or more of the following meanings: attempt to gain or maintain control in a situation via "bad guy" role, direct gratification of impulses, direct expression of hostility toward specific others or toward society.

15. <u>Perceived by Others in Some of the Following Ways</u>. Relatively integrated, non-neurotic, non-psychotic, unreliable, irresponsible, hedonistic, callous, hostile when cornered.

Treatment Plan for I-3 Mp:

1. <u>Goals</u>. Reduce fear of close, non-superficial relationships with others and of more direct expression of dependency needs; increase insight into use of projection and displacement; help him form a more accurate cause-and- effect connection between his own behavior and the response of others to reduce Mp's fear that being controlled by others (regardless of whom) equals "being destroyed;" change self-definition in direction of real (vs. imagined) interpersonal competence and worth, as part of reducing Mp's need to rely chiefly upon manipulation and to maintain a compensatory image of self as invincible, unapproachable, expertly elusive, or "able to care less" help boy Mp learn that adult males are not invariably or typically emasculated, pathetic or pitiful, "contemptible," or phony and that adult females are not invariably or typically "treacherous," pitiless or contemptuous toward males, distant or emotionally insulated; help girl Mp learn that adult females are not invariably weak, phony or helpless, and that adult males are not invariably rejecting, brutal or cold; increase social perceptiveness and prediction ability; increase interpersonal relating ability; change self-definition in direction of non-delinquency.

2. <u>Placement Plan</u>. Place Mp in setting where: an open communication network can be set up among parents (or substitutes) and Treatment Agent, manipulative behavior will not be rewarded, Mp will not be rejected as a result of his manipulative behavior (i.e. honest attempts will be made to be supportive and understanding as well as limiting and realistically demanding), independent action can be taken by parents (because of importance of <u>immediacy</u> of response) in line with an overall strategy agreed to by both parents and Agent. These conditions

can best be met in a group home or foster home of the defined characteristics. However, because of the interaction between the Mp and his natural parents, Mp may have to be placed in own home even though above conditions are not met. If so, eventual emancipation from the home remains a goal.

3. <u>Family Variables</u>. Agent should define "good parent" image to Mp's own or substitute parents as demonstrating <u>concern</u> for the Mp (rather than hostility or rejection) by imposing clear external structure. Encourage parents to handle Mp's behavior directly and immediately in firm, realistic and warm manner. Encourage parents to report to Agent treatment-relevant behavior and attitudes on part of the Mp. If Mp is in own home, support him in working through (discussing) destructive aspects of home situation without focusing blame on the parents. Agent should attempt to enhance the role or value of the Mp's same sex parent. Formal family group therapy (conjoint family therapy) appears inappropriate because of the destructiveness and inaccessibility of underlying feelings.

4. <u>Location of Community Supports</u>. There is little natural involvement of the Mp in the community because most community organizations reject him or her and Mps prefer unsupervised, unofficial activities. Encourage Mp's participation in any community organization, which relates to his abilities, or interests - recreational, athletic or artistic. Make use of Youth Corps training or manpower development programs when available. Agent should communicate directly with any community agency that is involved with Mp's family - welfare, school, etc so that services are not duplicated nor important areas ignored

5. <u>School Recommendations</u>. If Mp attends school, communication between Agent and school counselor or dean is crucial. School should be part of communications network set up around Mp so that his or her behavior will be known. If school attendance will mean an automatic failure (where either academic or behavioral demands are too great), tutoring or continuation school may be substituted or school program delayed or eliminated. Effort should be made to gear school program to Mp's academic or behavioral capabilities.

6. <u>Job Recommendations</u>. If of job age, help Mp find a job where his (superficial) interpersonal skills can be used in a way, which is rewarding to him but non-destructive to others (for example, grocery store clerk). Support job hunting and job keeping activities. Try to avoid failure experiences.

7. <u>Peer Group and Recreation Variables</u>. Since Mp is not trusted, he or she does not have long-term membership in natural peer group. Mp denies the need for close friends. Agent should attempt to build a Project peer group, comprised of Mps only, or Mps and Cfcs. Initially, the Mp is only supportive to other group members where payoff for himself is expected. Typically, Mps attack each other in the group, pointing out phoniness and "conning" behavior. Agent should encourage questioning but should teach group how to support individual members during crises. As the Mp begins to view the Agent (and, to a lesser extent, other Project personnel) as supportive and capable of meeting some of his needs, he begins to spend more time in activities at the treatment center. Agent should also encourage participation in outside activities where Mp can achieve some sense of adequacy and worth.

8. <u>Kind of Controls</u>. Mp must first learn that someone can and will control him. A communication network setup around the Mp (through family, schools, employer) can provide Agent with information necessary to control. External structure should be well defined with penalties for unacceptable behavior also well defined. A well-defined structure reveals the Mp's manipulative behavior to the Agent. Restrictions of his activities, use of extra work programs, and use of temporary detention are all useful in gaining Mp's attention. Very strict initial controls focuses the Mp's attention on the Agent and allows the Agent to begin communicating a message of concern for the youth.

9. <u>Agent Characteristics</u>. Agent should have the ability to empathize on the basis of nonverbal modes of communication and to utilize nonverbal modes in conveying empathy, and the ability to be aware of primitive drives and defenses against these. Even though he is empathic, the Agent should be able to maintain enough perspective to know when he is being "chumped". Agent should have the ability to exert friendly but firm parental control, ability to act promptly and appropriately in order to provide controls, ability to make definitive decisions and to act upon them. Agent should be able to understand the dependency needs underlying the Mp's compensatory "I am cool" facade and should be able to accept the Mp in spite of his manipulations. Agent must be willing to pick up the pieces of an almost demolished human being and hold the pieces together for a time - all this while preventing the Mp from demolishing others

10. <u>Treatment Methods</u>. Treatment of choice is Guided Group interaction, with emphasis on current interpersonal dealings and techniques for staying out of

trouble rather than on past history and reason (dynamics) for behavior. Attendance and participation in group should be mandatory. Three working sessions a week should be held; as a reward, an activity meeting can be substituted once in a while. Group may be composed of all Mps (with group size 4-8) or of Mps and Cfcs (with group size 7-11). If the two subtypes are combined in group, discussion of family problems is inhibited. No individual treatment is used initially, although some unscheduled individual contacts may take place around enrollment in school or home crisis; in these, Agent plays a buffer role. The first stage of treatment ends when the Mp is willing to admit that his way of doing things is not working and he is willing to try something else. In the second stage, the Mp is to some extent trying other-than-manipulative ways of relating with others. He will likely have numerous failures and hopefully some successes. As his proportion of successes increase, the issue of his leaving the group may be discussed in the group. The third stage of treatment begins when the group is no longer mandatory. In this stage, Agent may have some planned individual contacts with the Mp in which the Mp's job progress, marriage plans, specific interpersonal problems, etc. can be discussed. During this stage the Agent can, for the first time without threat to the youth, offer open emotional support and affection. Treatment with the Mp is long and goals are very difficult - sometimes impossible to reach.

11. <u>Suggested Techniques for Achieving Treatment Goals</u>. Create situation in which Mp's genuine feelings can be expressed and rewarded, regardless of content of the feelings. Demonstrate to him or her that the Agent is concerned about him by nonverbal demonstrations that real understanding of him does not lead to rejection and by willingness to control his behavior (implying that he

is worth the effort of controlling). Reduce stereotyping of others via failure to respond predictably to his manipulations based on stereotyped (undifferentiated) perception of Agent. Establish links between unpleasant results and his manipulations. Teach him to use direct, non-manipulative modes of reaching goals. Recognize Mp's unmet dependency needs; make more acceptable to the Mp the direct expression. of such needs, and meet the needs to the extent possible. By directly meeting some of the Mp's childlike dependency needs, reduce his reliance on such compensatory mechanisms as denial of needs and rejection of others as potential need-gratifiers. Demonstrate the acceptability of the notion of interdependence among individuals. By direct interaction demonstrate to Mp that Agent can cope with Mp's destructive parent (typically mother of the Mp boy and father of the Mp girl) without being destroyed. Help Mp develop skills which will redefine or enhance his masculine image (if a boy) or feminine image if a girl).

12. <u>Kind of Help the Agent Needs</u>. Since the course of treatment with the Mp is long and difficult, the program should offer the Agent rewards other than those arising from successful treatment. These rewards may be professional, including feedback from peers and supervisor regarding Agent's value as a treator, his skills, his imaginative approaches, One or two "change-of-pace" cases on the Agent's caseload offer rewards (Subtype Ci's make a good addition since they are typically interpersonally responsive.). Treatment supervisor should offer help in thinking through the specifics of treatment and in trying unorthodox treatment methods. Agent needs help in handling the Mp's hostility and in understanding the displaced from

the destructive parent) aspects of the Mp's anger. Group treatment consultation is an asset.

13. <u>Questions</u>. Should the major goal be to change the nature of the manipulator from delinquent and destructive to non-delinquent and socially acceptable? Or should the goal be changing the Mp into a non-manipulator?

My Supplemental Description

The following is a description of the Mp on the basis of field observations commonly made by the parents and spouses of Mps as well as many persons who have had unfavorable encounters with them.

I've spent much of my life working with Mps in just about every kind of social situation: in controlled residential settings, in field work, as an outreach worker, working directly with families in their homes, as a neighbor, friend, emergency out reach work, as a landlord when residents in my home, and as a leader of a small church with a prevalence of Mps. I've worked with all different age groups, from different socio-economic backgrounds, with different intellects, in different geographical areas, and from different cultural backgrounds. They're written about in nearly every book of the Bible. It's unbelievable how alike they are. I've traced the genealogy of some as far as four generations. I've repeatedly found, without exception, Mps propagate I-2s and I-3s and are the progeny of Mps. I'm convinced there's a genetic factor involved. Their core personalities and their basic behavior patterns are virtually identical.

They are extremely frightened people, despite a facade that gives the impression that they have "the world on a string." In a therapeutic setting, when feeling comfortable with the therapist, several have revealed to me that they are afraid of everything, especially people.

The Mps basic behavior patterns are primarily defensive. One of the keys to the problem is that they have very limited insight and foresight. They aren't able to understand themselves or others. They are unable to predict the behaviors of others and are unable to see that it is they themselves that cause their problems. This is why they depend on their formulas for operating and why they're so frightened. They project the blame to someone or something else because they are unable to realize that their behavior affects others; the only rational explanation they can perceive is that the problem has to be outside of themselves. This is also why they reject any input that might change their position. They're unable to internalize anything that might help them change and are afraid that any change might make matters worse. They have difficulty accepting the fact that they may be wrong. Even when confronted with empirical evidence, they rarely, if ever, admit they are wrong, or that someone else might be right.

They suffer much abuse as children, which leads many agents to believe their behavior was environmentally determined. This is an erroneous assumption, as determined by field observations. They have relatively no conscience, nor compassion. They are unable to see that the problems they have, they bring on themselves. They project the blame to other people, things or circumstances. They're very skilled pathological liars. They believe their own lies and if their scheming doesn't work, as they planned, they fabricate lies, or distort the truth, to make it appear as though it had.

They are terrified when their plans don't work; if they lose control of others, or circumstances, they become extremely frustrated and have what appear to be psychotic episodes. That's usually when they come to the attention of an agency, who then diagnoses them as manic-depressives, or more commonly, bipolar.

I believe this is a misdiagnosis. Human behavior is logically illogical; there is a logic to it but it defies normal logic and reasoning. With the manic-depressive there is no overt rationale for their mood swings, giving rise to the conclusion, that it is due to a neurological problem. Whereas with the Mp, through analysis it can be found that the Mp is reacting to a loss of control of a person or circumstance, which is not a neurological problem; nor is it a psychological problem per se, but a physiological problem. As stated earlier, it is an SPD, (Sensory Processing Disorder) that accounts for their insensitivity to their physical and social environment. However, where SPD studies suggest a neurological problem, which may be true of some clients, in this section of treatment strategy, it appears that the Mp can increase the sensitivity of certain sensory receptors. Though he may appear to be emotionally insulated, as though by choice, in reality he's simply insensitive to the subtle stimuli of his physical and social environment.

I believe this is the basis for his fear. He has an underdeveloped ego. The ego is the aggregate of all of our life experiences. Without certain functional sensory receptors, the Mp is unable to experience many of the stimuli needed for the development of a normal, or sophisticated, ego.

This I believe accounts for the statement that the Mp does not appear to learn from experience: *"Functions socially from a rigidly closed frame of reference that is self-reinforcing and consistently rejecting of information that might modify its structure."*

With an ego of limited experiences, he develops his identity on the bases of what ego he has. From his perspective, anything that might influence the ego can destroy his identity. Without an identity he ceases to exist, which is a real threat from his perspective, or anyone's for that matter.

People who are or have been closely associated with Mps describe them as "control freaks." This agrees with his own self-concept that *"overestimates potential of these formulas (conning and conforming) as a means of being able to control others and bring about the desired outcome in any situation."*

As for the nature of the Mp's crisis being *a result of his application of formula for operating, failure to work, or a result of perceived threat to his ability remain in control (of self, others, situations)*, in an effort to justify their own self-image, or to alienate others, the Mp finds it necessary to degrade others. Mps are narcissistic and masters at provoking people. They tend to fear intimacy with others; they attract people, but if the relationship borders on intimacy, or if the person is no longer useful for their purposes, they rapidly destroy the relationship. People are merely objects to use.

The only variations I've seen in the behavior of Mps is the intensity of their aggressiveness. Their destructiveness can range from just malicious gossip to bizarre and violent crimes. In either case someone gets hurt. Their favorite targets for abuse are 1-2s and Cfms. They're bullies; they constantly use intimidation and coercion to control people and to identify potential victims. As bullies, they are selective in their victims, choosing only those that they see as weaker than themselves. This is what I think accounts for the variations in the intensity of their aggressiveness. Occasionally they will find I-4s they can victimize. They prey on either their neurosis and guilt feelings, or on their rescuing behavior with the "Poor Me" game. Depending on the condition of the victim, they can do severe damage by intensifying their neurosis, and to some they may even induce psychosis.

They have a conflict between their need for intimacy and their fear of it. As mentioned earlier, due to their interpersonal relationship maturity level, they function socially as a preadolescent. As a preadolescent, as with all preadolescents, they are somewhat bewildered in regards to heterogeneous and homogeneous relationships. Preadolescents are striving to develop from homogeneous relationships to heterogeneous relationships as a normal developmental task. The Mp, however, seems unable to make the transition. Thus, the conflict continues. Of the many Mps I've observed, they seem to resolve the conflict in one of two ways: they continue to prefer homogeneous relationships and thus, homosexual relationships, or they may develop heterosexual relationships for the purpose of manipulating and degrading those of the opposite sex. Thus their sensory needs are met, but they continue to avoid intimate relationships of any depth.

Another aspect of their aggressiveness occurs when *he perceives the power of another as likely to have an impact on him. Fights back against power both subtly and obviously. Important to his self image to be seen as in control of himself and having power over others.* They are masters of non-verbal cues. They use them quite effectively in controlling others. In marriage counseling, to determine the truth and to enable the spouse of the Mp to communicate his or her view, I've found it to be most effective if the spouse turns their back to the Mp, and to insist the Mp "shut up" and let the spouse speak for himself or herself. In judgmental situations, such as court hearings between spouses, or in various hearings where both spouses are involved, the non-Mp spouse is advised to sit in a position where they are not able to see the Mp. Frequently this will frustrate the Mp because he views this as a loss of control and will often become aggressive and show his true behavior.

His social functioning is so rigid it is highly predictable. His behavior is so predictable that specific techniques can successfully thwart his destructiveness with or without attacking his ego.

His favorite psychological games are as follows:

Poor Me: He uses this game to induce others, particularly "rescuers" to meet his dependency needs.

Yes, But: This game is used to reject any input that might influence his perception of his behavior

> **Rapo:** This is a seductive game that promises
> sexual pleasures, but in reality is used to
> ultimately degrade persons of the opposite sex.

Let's You and Him Fight: This is one of the Mp's favorite games. They seem to thrive on creating problems between people. This seems to be used as a control technique and also as a means to degrade others in an effort to raise their own self-esteem. When they have identified someone that they perceive as having some influence over their control, they enlist the help of another person to do their "dirty work" of attack. In enlisting the help of another, they describe their victim's behavior with distorted and fabricated data. This induces a helper to attack the victim unjustly. This, in turn, creates animosity between the victim and the helper.

Uproar: This is a variation of the "Lets You and Him Fight" game. In this game the Mp tries to enlist as many people as he can to attack his victim. When, collectively, they realize they've been "duped" by the Mp, the Mp is rejected. In the meanwhile there has been much confusion and contention among those enlisted to help.

I'm Only Trying to Help You: This is another method they use to control people as well as degrade them. They speak with authority implying that they have a solution for people's problems. In reality they seldom do. Though they really believe that they have all the answers, they seldom do because of their limited insight and limited foresight.

Suicide: Suicide is a form of the "Poor Me" game. It is used as a manipulative technique to gain sympathy and capitalize on that to obtain some specific goal. This is usually a calculated risk. They usually know just how far they can go to give the impression that they are serious and yet stop just in time before any irreparable damage occurs. Occasionally they miscalculate.

Conversation Control: They seem to use conversational control in an effort to convince others of their superior intellect, which is really a sham. If confronted with facts they'll change the subject quickly and turn to some trivia. On the surface it appears that they are attempting to convince you of their knowledge of all subjects, especially those you are not familiar with. I believe the underlying motive is simple control of your attention and the social interaction needed without knowledge of alternatives.

Learned Mp Behavior

Occasionally I came across a youth who had many Mp symptoms and had been diagnosed as such. In working with them, however, I noted that they had insight and a conscience, which are contrary to the Mp personality. On investigation, it appeared that they had older, Mp, half-siblings, or they had an Mp stepparent.

Another common characteristic of the Mp that can make diagnosis difficult is that when things are going their way, they can be wonderful people, very generous and very helpful, and they can give the impression that they are concerned about others. Not knowing the characteristics of the Mp leaves people very vulnerable to the Mp's aggressive behavior. They can turn on friends very suddenly for no apparent or logical reason. Only careful analysis of the circumstances can deduce any logical or rational reason for their behavior. I believe that, in most spousal and child abuse cases, an Mp can be found to be the abuser.

The following is a verbatim dialog I had with the mother of a forty-eight-year-old Mp daughter, which can illustrate some of the Mp's description:

"...this makes me wonder about what kind of a man his father was? The way you describe your grandchildren makes me guess that two are Mps and two are the passive types (Cfms) that I mentioned before. What are their parents like? Were any of the parents Mps? They have a compulsive need to control everyone and everything, that's why I asked about J-1s father; I thought he might be an Mp."

"I did not like my husband's father. He had a quick temper and could be abusive. When we were first married he was wanting help to move some cattle and everyone was busy but me. So I tried to help, but the cattle got away I didn't run fast enough I guess and he started cussing me out. I had never been treated that way before and I threw my stick at him and went to the house. Nothing was ever said about it and he was pretty silent around me. And I avoided him. Before he died he had a stroke and was partially paralyzed. They lived at our house for several months. But he was confined to the bedroom. His mother went to live with a brother. I know he drank quite a bit and ruled his family with a iron hand and wasn't above kicking or hitting them. Once at the county fair I saw him come out of the fortune teller's camper that was behind her tent. How much of that went on I don't know. He never took his wife to public things. His mother had four boys, all alcoholics, and she always had to have a girl to help with the house work and such. But she lived into her nineties. Guess what I am trying to get at about my grandchildren is, two are as straightlaced and good as can be, two are wild and sometimes out of control."

My guess, without personal observance, is that two are Cfms and two are Mps. And note the
statement, *"He never took his wife to public things."* They like to isolate their spouses, or mates. They demand an accounting of their spouses whereabouts and now, in the cell phone age, they frequently call the spouses to check on their activities. The spouses feel they're being spied on. On the other hand, neutral observers are reminded of a child constantly seeking mother's whereabouts. This is a demonstration of their fear and dependency as well as rationale for their need to control. They are afraid they can't handle the various situations they're faced with so they use people to do the tasks they feel inept at doing themselves. (This is quite apparent in their "uproar game.") However, instead of allowing their helper to determine the means and the goals, they attempt to impose their own prescription for the means and ends.

Re: Daughter J1: Mp

"When we lived together she definitely tried to control. And was only friends with me or her dad never both at the same time…"

…

"After the divorce she lived with her dad. But never lost contact with me. Would come and visit. They had an interesting relationship. Both controlling the other one. He controlled the money and if she wanted to buy anything that wasn't on the list she had to call him and get an okay. But on the other hand, she would shut herself in her room and refuse to cook, or whatever he wanted. I never knew what caused her to shut the door. But now she does the same to me; it's a seasonal thing with me and this winter she hasn't cut me off completely. Will answer my email sometimes. She always feels she is smarter than everyone else, and usually is. She was always trying to outsmart her counselors and was pretty successful at it. Her last one was her equal, but they didn't accomplish much, except he did get her to admit she used food to adjust her moods as she wanted to. A few things like that. I'm not sure whether her thinking is "get the other person before they get me." Seems to be more "to get what I want." Her attitude about the world is "be indestructible and they can't hurt me no matter what." She has a wall built around herself. She cannot express her feeling at all. Once in a while something will bolt out and than she shuts it off right then. She definitely rejects any dependency on anyone else. She used to have short relationships with people but has shut down the outside world and except for business she has to do, stays pretty much to herself."

Effective Treatment of the Mp

As stated in the I-Level Theory treatment plans, the treatment of the Mp is long, and goals are very difficult or sometimes impossible to reach. Treating the Mp is more difficult than the other personalities described. In my experience, I had little to no success in treating the Mps in the community. They rarely seek help. They are resistant to change. They try to give overall impression of feeling that their way of life is comfortable, effective and satisfactory. They reject the idea of change in themselves, their attitudes and situations.

However, I was able to control my relationship with them. Unfortunately, this didn't extend to their relationships with others. We did have a high degree of success in treating the Mp at O.H. Close using the basic treatment plan.

Initially I attempted to develop a universal treatment plan for all delinquent youths; however, with the introduction of the I-Level theory and their goal of differential treatment I looked for the specific needs of each of the I-Level types. I later came to realize that the universal treatment plan that had been devised was actually beneficial to each of the types. Each type was able to benefit according to his individual needs. The treatment plan was eventually refined to ten specific objectives, which the wards were expected to make an effort to do. They were as follows:

1. Helping others
2. Individual counseling
3. Small group counseling
4. Large group meeting
5. Indoor activities
6. Outdoor activities
7. School
8. Living unit cleanup
9. Peer relationships
10. Staff relationships

At the time, my intent was to provide as many opportunities as I could for the wards to learn social skills in various situations. This was based on the assumption that given enough meaningful learning experiences they could progress to the next I-level, as suggested in the I-level report. However, on the basis of further studies and experience, I concluded that they weren't able to progress to the next I-level, but were able to function better, improve their interpersonal relationship skills, increase their sensitivity to their physical and social environment and reduce their aggressiveness.

In the case of the Mps, I've traced the genealogy of some as far as four generations. I've repeatedly found, without exception, Mps propagate I-2s and I-3s and are the progeny of Mps. I'm convinced there's a genetic factor involved. Their core personalities and their basic behavior patterns are virtually identical.

At one point we thought the Mps were supersensitive. If an event occurred where someone was severely hurt, they tended to overreact. At the same time they appeared to be insensitive to certain aspects of both their physical and social environments. Further observations suggested that they were unable to perceive subtle stimuli, suggesting that the thresholds of certain sensory receptors were too narrow to perceive any stimuli of a minimal magnitude. This I believe is related to Skinner's statement, which you will recall by now as follows:

> *The magnitude of a stimulus is the intensity which is barely sufficient to elicit a response. In a reflex, the magnitude of the response varies with the magnitude of the stimulus. The more intense the stimulus the greater the magnitude of the response and the shorter the latency of reflex.*

As, has been demonstrated by many people who have lost the sensitivity of one sense, they are able to compensate by increasing the sensitivity of other senses. I believe that we had inadvertently increased the sensitivity of the youths on our units. Though the Mp may appear to be emotionally insulated, as though by choice, in reality he's simply insensitive to the subtle stimuli of his physical and social environment.

Reviewing the descriptions of the Mps with the assumption that they have certain dysfunctional receptors suggests a validity of this assumption. If they can't perceive the stimulus, it doesn't exist for them. Without these perceptions certain realities don't exist. Attempts to discuss reality with them is virtually impossible and most often leads to an argument. Arguments with an Mp are counterproductive. The Mp uses arguments to try to force you to accept his way of thinking and to cover his ignorance. Arguments are merely a means to degrade others and reinforce their self-concept of being smarter than others.

It's also a control technique. I've found that by saying, "You might be right," turning around and walking away will counter the argument. Another method I use is to simply state the truth, turn my back and walk away. This is related to chained behavior patterns, described by Berne:

> *The overt manifestations of social intercourse are called transactions. Typically these occur in chains: a transactional stimulus from X elicits a transactional response from Y; this response becomes a stimulus for X, and X's response in turn becomes a new stimulus for Y. Transactional Analysis is concerned with the analysis of such chains.*

The Mp has such a rigid behavior pattern that by not responding as he anticipates leaves him at a loss as to what to do next. The chain is broken. Turning your back also blocks his next move of employing non-verbal cues. Of the two methods mentioned, I usually prefer the first method in my personal contacts. In a controlled setting I use both methods, depending on the circumstances.

They simply can't understand regardless of their intellect.

I believe the 10-point program addressed this insensitivity. Helping others and each of the counseling activities increased their awareness of others as well as their needs. Their cleanup activities were extremely scrutinized by the staff who pointed out minute details that had been missed.

They were expected to respect the games they used for their indoor activities. Mps are generally destructive to toys and various pieces of equipment. Equipment that was being mistreated was confiscated, and when the wards complained, they were told to bring it up at the community meeting. At the meetings the pros and cons related to the care of the equipment were discussed and the wards were encouraged to decide how they would handle it by consensus.

The equipment they used for their outdoor activities was treated with much the same disrespect without insight, nor foresight. When they were through with the activity they would simply drop the equipment or throw it away to be picked up by another unit.

At times I would use some dramatic action to gain their attention. At one time, after all the youths had returned to the dayroom, I would pick up any equipment that was left out and put it in a corner behind my desk. This collection could be observed through the window from the dayroom. When I had finally collected all of their outdoor equipment they began to ask what my intentions were and if they could have the equipment returned. They were encouraged to bring it up at the meeting. In the meeting it was pointed out that we had limited resources, and that if they didn't take care of the equipment there would be none and no way to replace it. I also pointed out that I wasn't their mother who picked up after them. They were old enough and capable enough to pick up after themselves. It was pointed out that they knew what I would do and that I wanted to know what they would do to regain and retain the use of the equipment. At the conclusion of the meeting, as with other meetings, they determined, by consensus, how they would handle the care of the equipment.

I also expected them to respond the first time I said anything. Mps, like many other children, delay their response to parental requests for a calculated number of times. They know how many times their parents will make the same request before they act on it. I used different tones of voice to reinforce a positive response, or to reinforce avoidance behavior. In either case the desired behavior was always reinforced with a positive generalized reinforcer.

I strived to create, as best I could, a clinic-like environment in an attempt to determine what worked and what didn't work. Consistency was essential. Our rigid time structuring played an important role in achieving this end. The youths were able to anticipate what would occur each hour of the day. This aided their adaptation period and thus increased their rate of learning in the various treatment programs. Their behavior was shaped by using respondent and operant conditioning with reinforced avoidance behavior, much positive reinforcement with generalized reinforcers, and various forms of counseling.

Counseling was not effective with the Mp, initially. But, as time progressed and they became more sensitive to their environment, their awareness increased and they gained some benefit from counseling.

Mps, like everyone else, are dominated by a need for sensory stimulation. When an Mp approaches, he is seeking stimulation. When you break the anticipated chain, his need is left unmet. His response is dependent upon his relationship with you.

If your initial contact is warm and friendly and reinforced with generalized reinforcers, conditioning will begin. On the other hand if your relationship has been based on contention, sympathy, or submission, the extinction process must be utilized. Arguments must be avoided using the methods mentioned above. The minute you find yourself caught up in an argument, you've "been had." He's in control and you're reinforcing this behavior. If his requests are denied, he may go off and pout, in an effort to gain your sympathy (the Poor Me Game) and submission to his request. It is best to ignore this move, leaving his need for sensory stimulation unmet. He will soon feel the effects of the unmet need and think to gain your attention in a more appropriate way. This change of attitude is best met by not mentioning the previous attitude and reinforcing all positive efforts. In other instances a temper tantrum may follow a denial of his requests.

The temper tantrums of an Mp are much different than those of an I 2. They can be extremely destructive and extremely dangerous. In many cases they need to be restrained. In many cases it may be easier said than done. In my encounters I had the advantage of being athletic and physically strong. I only used my strength as a last alternative. Whenever possible I would try to maneuver them into a chair, preferably a large soft chair. It's nearly impossible for them to rise out of a chair against even a slight amount of counterforce. (You have to spread your legs to avoid getting kicked, though.)

I'm not sure whether all Mps are violent-prone. From my observations, it has seemed that it is dependent upon the physical size of the desired victim. In other cases they have managed to restrain themselves, in fear of authoritative intervention. I've also observed Mps restrain themselves when their intended victim is stronger and revert to threats and degrading remarks to intimidate their victim, such as a spouse. At the same time, these same Mps will physically abuse a smaller and weaker child.

I've also seen Mps, who have restrained themselves for fear of authoritative intervention, delegate authority over their children to their spouse. If the children don't respond to the authority, the Mp can then blame the spouse and thus deny any personal loss of control.

In any event, when an Mp is throwing a tantrum, whenever possible, it is best for spouses, partners and children to escape and seek help. I believe that a vast number of spousal and child abuse cases can be attributed to an Mp.

Following an episode where a spouse or child is severely abused by an Mp, the Mp often expresses remorse, seeks forgiveness and strives for reconciliation. There may be two explanations for this response. One may be that the severity of what he has done is perceptible to him and stimulates some compassion for his victim. This is the impression he gives; but I'm not so sure his motivation is compassion, but rather fear of rejection from those he depends on.

Let's look at some of the I-Level statements about the Mp again:

Will not allow himself to consummate (or is fearful of consummating) relationships in which he is in any way dependent upon another person. Denies and rejects dependency needs as part of himself.

Perceives others as being unwilling to meet his dependency needs. Assumes that others will try to "use" him to their own advantage.

People are merely objects to use.

Believes that others will not meet his needs unless he "takes it (the need satisfier) away" from them.

I believe these statements are contraindicated by the Mps behavior. The Mps behavior indicates a very strong dependency. It also indicates a conflict between two diametrically opposed forces. On the one hand they need to control, and on the other, recognition that there are some things they can't understand and consequently can't achieve. This seems to be their motive for manipulation. They manipulate to maintain their identity as a controller and they manipulate to have others meet needs that they can't meet themselves. The needs they aren't able to meet themselves are related to the dysfunctional sensory receptors that are unable to perceive the data needed to meet their need. Attempting to teach them the data they need, through their intellect, is like trying to explain the shape of something to a blind person. They seem to respond best through their senses. If a blind person can run their fingers over the shape, they can perceive the shape more accurately than they can by merely having it described to them. Without this understanding of the Mp, most people perceive the Mps dependency as just plain laziness. It's not, but over time they many simply give up and accept their lot in life.

One 13-year-old Mp that was brought to my attention was able to express this concept quite clearly following a football injury. He was a bright youth, but very dependent and very frightened for no apparent reasons. Reassurance did very little to help him overcome his fears. He loved to play football and was good at it. Football entails many stimuli of a strong magnitude. But he sustained a hip injury and at the insistence of his doctor and his mother he had to be placed on the injured reserve group and told not to play football until he was well. He got furious with the doctor and his mother and made a statement that pretty well describes what I've mentioned. He said, "I finally found something I was good at and you won't let me do it!"

The point I'm making is that with strong stimuli he could respond very well; he compared this with his failings in areas dependent on stimuli of a low magnitude.

I believe the Mp can be most effectively treated in a controlled residential setting. In using a modified therapeutic community, the wards are accountable to each other and thus help each other become aware of stimuli, in their physical and social environment, that are of a low magnitude. Increasing the thresholds of dysfunctional sensory receptors can enable the Mp to perceive the data necessary for him to assume responsibility for his behavior and thus reduce his dependency. As his dependency diminishes, so also does his aggressiveness. Reducing his dependency in turn reduces his need to control others. The basic program focuses on increasing their awareness of stimuli of a low magnitude. I don't believe that the Mp can experience enough meaningful learning experiences outside of a controlled residential setting, where every hour of his day is directed toward increasing his awareness.

Prior to the Mp treatment program at O.H. Close, there was little optimism regarding successful treatment of the Mp. The results of the basic program of the Mp unit had the lowest recidivism rate of any unit in the state. My own caseload had a 0% recidivism rate in a 2 1/2 year period, as reported by the CYA parole division. Though my rationale and assumptions may be erroneous and considered an oversimplification, the results were undeniable.

CHAPTER 6

The I-4

General Characteristics
(1966 Revision)

Ways of Perceiving the World:

1. <u>Internalized Standards</u>. Has internalized a set of ideals,
    standards and values by which he judges his and others'
    behavior. Consciously feels remorseful, inadequate or
    guilty when he does not measure up to these standards
    or shows some evidence of discomfort or conflict
    regarding standards.

2. <u>Differentiates Himself from the Stereotyped Norm</u>.
    Has a sense of self, which he differentiates from the
    conventional or stereotyped standard. Sees himself
    and wants others to see him as non-average, unique,
    different from others his own age. Begins to evaluate
    himself along certain dimensions as better or worse
    than others.

3. <u>Status Concerns</u>. Has status and prestige concerns. Wants to get ahead and make something of himself. Wants recognition from those he admires - recognition of his special or different qualities; i.e., his ideals or interests, his potentialities or accomplishments.

4. <u>Identification</u>. Tries to model himself after those he looks up to, those whom he sees as being special or accomplished - wanting to be like them in actions, attitudes or attributes. (In a negative identification pattern, may wish to be "just the opposite of" a non-admired model.) Goal and plans are strongly influenced by those he admires (or, less frequently, by those whom he hates or for whom he has contempt).

5. <u>Some Perception or Causal Factors</u>. Some perception of the factors which impinge on him both from within and without and some perception of the interplay between these forces. Potential for considerable insight into leanings, dynamics, cause and effect.

6. <u>Some Perception of Needs and Motives in Self and Others</u>. Shows some ability to look for or understand reasons for behavior. May see his actions and the actions of others as motivated by feelings and past events. Able to perceive feelings and motivations which are not just like his own. May be only poorly able to describe this perception, especially if of low intelligence or culturally deprived.

7. <u>Some Ability to Look into the Future</u>. Able to think about the future with personal meaning and plan in relatively realistic ways (including certain impossibilities for himself), even though distortion may be present. May worry or be playful about the future (even though not always able to carry through on plans). He can

perceive that self and circumstances can be different several years from now, and he can decide some of the possibilities. Oriented toward goals.

Ways of Responding to the World:

8. <u>Relationship Ability</u>. Shows some ability to enter into two-way (reciprocal) relationships of more than just a dependency or supportive nature. Able to relate with another person in terms of the individualized needs, feelings, standards or ideals held by themselves and the other person.

9. <u>Concept of Accountability is Meaningful to Him</u>. Able to assume some responsibility for self and others. May recognize the need to be responsible but may be unable to carry this out.

10. <u>Capacity to Delay Response to Immediate Stimuli</u>. Because he can respond to stimuli which are not immediately present and because he can anticipate the way in which he may later judge his present action, he shows some capacity to delay response to immediate stimuli.

I-4, NX and NA Characteristics
1966 Revision (Incomplete)

Ways of Perceiving the World:

1. <u>Rigidified Guilt</u>. Guilt based on long past internalization of childlike perceptions of identification figure. Internalization of the "bad me," and resulting "negative life script." Investment in maintaining "bad me" concept. Initially, worker may see primarily a defense

against guilt - compensating "I am special" defenses and/or overlays of guilt about more recent inadequacies (Nonachievement in school, inadequate social skills, inability to fill in for absent parent, etc.)

2. <u>Non-Self</u>. May characterize aspects of his past and present behavior as non-self, not like him, incomprehensible to him, ego-alien.

3. <u>Anxiety Re: Self</u>. Anxiety is not situationally determined but rather is constantly with him. Felt anxiety is typically related to perception of self as inadequate, to identification conflicts or to interpersonal difficulties.

4. <u>Wants to Change in Order to Improve</u>. Wants to be a better person, to hurt less himself, or to stop hurting others. May have plans for self-improvement or may be asking for help either to achieve a new personality integration or to increase the efficiency or protective value of his neurotic mode of functioning.

Ways of Responding to the World:

5. <u>Delinquency as Part of the Neurosis</u>. The delinquency may be the acting out of a family problem or the acting-out of a long-standing internal conflict, particularly a conflict involving the internalization of a parental or authority image. Delinquent behavior has some private meaning and does not represent simply a material gain (or the gain is not the object of the act), or simply response to cultural or peer pressure.

6. <u>Selectivity in Friendships</u>. If he or she has friends, there is some selectivity (other than juxtaposition) to his friendships. Relationships, when present, are with

specific other person, as opposed to having someone to fulfill the friendship role. May be a social isolate.

Characteristics Differentiating NA from NX:
(Incomplete)

Compared to the NX, the Na;

1. Is less differentiated with respect to his inner life, his feelings and those of others.

2. Has a compensating self-definition as adequate, assumed to be a cover-up for the "bad me" - with little or no connection between the two levels at intake.

3. Has a greater need to perceive self as autonomous. Consciously wants others to recognize, accept and value him in terms of this image of autonomy, and is likely to interpret attempted control by others as rejection (of his adequacy or autonomy).

4. More typically acts out to avoid feelings of anxiety.

5. Wants to <u>overcome</u> problems more than to <u>resolve</u> problems. Focuses on mastery of present life situations and difficulties.

6. Tends to dichotomize rather than dimensionalize others, especially with regard to value-loaded characteristics. For example, in terms of his values, the Na can list "the good people" and "the bad people."

7. Is more intensely angry both at and below the surface.

8. Uses projection (of the unacceptable parts of the self-image) as a major defense mechanism.

9. Is not ready for insight therapy.

10. Is not perceived by others as emotionally disturbed, neurotic, anxious.

Treatment Plan for I-4 NA:
(1966 Revision)

1. <u>Goals</u>. Long-range goals include: elimination of delinquency; reduction or resolution of internal conflicts, and of use of defense mechanisms and pseudo-independent manner of relating in ways which are harmful to self or others; more accurate perception of who he is and really wants to be, in contrast to perception of self in terms of definitions and roles he has gotten or accepted from others for reasons of security and defense, or partial and indirect gratification; changed self-image in direction of sense of personal worth and of basic acceptability to others and to potential worth (as a mature person, not as a "bad" person) to others; greater awareness of actual (vs. imaginary) limitations and needs; ability to relax and not need to always "run;" movement toward I-5 (increased perceptual differentiation of self and others, increased self knowledge, increased awareness of complex patterns in others); increased level of functioning (improved role definitions) in school, job, family and other relevant areas. Short-term (immediate) goals include: encouragement of Na to find out who the Agent is, who the group is or what the rules of the game are, before he is forced to make a treatment commitment; establishment of treatment contract between Na and Agent or between family and Agent; moratorium on acting-out behavior; specified and agreed-upon plan regarding initial placement, job, school, limits, etc.

2. <u>Placement Plan</u>. Place Na at home initially, if parents are willing to accept his or her return and if the Na is willing. Placement at home is essential if family group therapy (conjoint family therapy) is the treatment of choice. If Na's own family is unavailable or if they are unable to or unwilling to modify problem-producing interactions, Na may be placed in foster or group home temporarily or permanently. Real emancipation from the home can only begin when the Na himself recognizes that this is the only (or best) solution. Characteristics of an out-of-home placement appropriate for the Na are: Home offers initial emphasis on open communication and explanation of motives and intentions when appropriate to eliminate or head off misinterpretations by the Na; home provides a base from which Na can work on resolution of internal conflicts, emancipation and identity problems; home allows the Na some independence; parents can relate flexibly to the Na on a closeness-distance dimension; parents can permit the Na to take the initiative in determining their relationship; parents must be tolerant of nonverbal testing, accepting and non-threatening; parents must be permissive regarding Na's continued relationship with his own family; and parents should be able to pick up nonverbal cues regarding the Na's emotional state and communicate these to the Agent.

3. <u>Family Treatment</u>. Formal family group therapy (conjoint family therapy) should be treatment of choice if: (a) mother and father figures and other relevant family members are available; (b) all family members agree to the treatment; and (c) individual contacts between the Na and Agent are unnecessary. Under these conditions, the family accepts the responsibility for the Na as with any other family member; i.e., responsibility for decisions regarding school, job, and behavior. Agent

should concentrate on the treatment content and family communication and feelings, and play down assignment of the Na to the role of identified-patient. Less formal family treatment (family conferences) can occur; without the above conditions being met. In the latter instance, individual and group methods should also be used, and the goal may be emancipation from the home. Family treatment may facilitate the emancipation process. Since the Na may try to re-enact his family problem in a foster or group home setting, the Agent should offer support to the substitute parents via understanding and suggested techniques for dealing with Na.

4. <u>Location of Community Supports</u>. Typically, not relevant to the Na's delinquency problem at intake. Agent may get information for the Na and encourage participation in community activities as treatment progresses.

5. <u>School and Job Recommendations</u>. With the Na, the first problem to be solved relates to the neurotic aspects of the delinquency; therefore, school or job is a secondary issue. The significance of these activities as aspects of the initial plan varies from Na to Na. School and job requirements may be control issues relevant to the initial phases of treatment. These factors become more important in their own right in the development of individual potential as treatment progresses.

6. <u>Leisure Time Activities</u>. Project-sponsored activities may be used as a supplement to specific treatment methods. Offer constructive activities which are satisfying to the Na and which will meet status needs in terms of the standards of the larger culture. Involve the Na in sports where he can compete with himself; e.g., golf, weight lifting, track. Team responsibility is difficult for the Na to handle.

7. <u>Peer Group Variables</u>. If an individual Na plan is based on individual psychotherapy primarily, he or she may be encouraged to participate with a peer group of I-4s in social activities in order to increase fund of interpersonal skills and satisfactions. Na's may be asked to assist with lower maturity subtypes as a means of enhancing the Na's ego identity and sense of value to others.

8. <u>Kind of Controls</u>. Although the major focus is on internal, psychological controls, initially external controls may be necessary. The content of the controls should be reality-based and should coincide with the Na's expectations. Inner controls should be encouraged. Agent should play it straight with the Na and demand the same from him or her - this interaction acts as a control. Issues of control may be used therapeutically by the Agent for purposes of communicating support and concern. Na may raise issues relating to trust, personal acceptance, the impact of own impulses or counter dependency by deliberately challenging the Agent's rules or personal standards (stated or unstated). Areas of conflict between the Na and the Agent should be carefully chosen so that the Na may sometimes "win the argument" without being lost to the program. The content of the issues should, nevertheless, be real and important to both the Na and the Agent.

9. <u>Kind of Agent</u>. Agent should be internally-oriented and comfortable with identity as a treator. He should not fear emotional disturbance and should have understanding of and respect for neurotic and coping defenses. Agent should be patient, able to persevere, not easily distracted from a treatment focus by Na's defenses. He should have considerable self-knowledge regarding dynamics and be able to handle issues of transference and counter

transference. He should be willing to make himself open (emotionally available) to the Na. An open, two-way communication system on a feeling level offers, not only a source of support for insight development, but also a ready source of information for identification. Additionally, this provides the Na with a basis for reality testing throughout the treatment process. The Agent should be an individual of personality complexity, one who has resolved or greatly reduced any major personal problems. If the Agent has not experienced personal difficulties in his own life, he may be less sensitive to the intensity of the Na's feelings, his needs and his limitations.

10. <u>Treatment Methods</u>. Major methods are individual psychotherapy, group psychotherapy and/or family group therapy (conjoint family therapy), with an emphasis on the development of insight into conflicts, personal capacities and family problems. Initial structure, activity groups, school tutoring and environmental manipulation may be used as appropriate in line with overall goals.

11. <u>Suggested Techniques for Achieving Goals</u>. Encourage the Na to explore the environment and, at the same time, permit him to experience the consequences of these exploratory actions. Provide him with opportunities to practice a variety of responses to social situations. Allow the Na time to integrate roles and choices with other aspects of his overall adjustment pattern - his areas of actual strength and limitations, his emerging picture of himself and of his changing standards and ideals. Regardless of the type of psychotherapy, timing and level of interpretation are very important - with decisions to be made on the basis of Na's ego strength, consciousness of conflicts, etc. Focus on symptoms (delinquency) is useless or worse; Agent should concentrate on underlying

feelings and problems. This should not preclude the Agent's introducing realistic initial structure, not only as a support, but also as a means of meeting the expectations of the Na in this regard. Considerable emotional support for the Na should be forthcoming from the Agent while conflicts are being resolved, particularly during crises. Emotional support should be offered in such a way as to avoid threatening the Na's conscious self-image as independent and problem-free.

12. <u>Kind of Help the Agent Needs</u>. Consultation and supervision regarding dynamics of cases, and counter transference reactions, is essential. Agent needs a source of support for continual reevaluation of self in a Creator role; assistance in continually evaluating the Na's potential for growth, the Agent's level of interpretation, timing, etc. Training and consultation are needed regarding the specific treatment methods being applied.

13. <u>Questions</u>. How can the Agent establish meaningful initial structure and avoid being seen by the Na as focusing on symptoms? How can the agent estimate the timing of removal of the tangible supportive structure so that Na can test his own controls?

Characteristics Differentiating NX from NA:
(Incomplete)

Compared to the Na, the Nx:

1. Is more tolerant of feeling anxious.

2. Is more able to anticipate consequences of behavior or expression of impulses (hurt to others, guilt re: self).

3. Appears motivated to search for, and conceptualize, some of the causes of his discomfort, feelings about himself, etc.

4. Is more comfortable with perception of self as dependent and needing help.

5. Is openly critical of his own present inadequacies, combined with a "I am special" self presentation. Description of present inadequacies may represent cover-up for primitive "bad me" perception. Some connection between the two levels is available to consciousness.

6. Can verbalize the relationship between his feelings of discomfort (as well as feelings about self-worth) and his subsequent behavior.

7. Can make an open connection between hurting others and his self-image or his ways of coping.

8. Has anxiety which delinquent acting-out alone cannot handle. Neurotic symptoms represent compromises between impulses and repressive forces (conscience, self-image). A wide range of fear or anxiety laden, consciously unpleasant and unwanted symptoms may be present insomnia, nightmares, phobias, etc.

9. Uses introjections as a prominent defense mechanism. Reliance upon this mechanism often leads others to see the Nx as having a highly developed conscience (being filled with remorse) or a severe superego. Nx accepts the idea of punishing himself or otherwise paying for the damage or hurt he has caused.

10. Appears distressed, unhappy or discontented in attitude, appearance or manner. Nx is perceived by others as

anxious, nervous, depressed, discouraged, defensive, emotionally disturbed, seclusive, "oddball." He or she is also perceived as sensitive and reachable.

Treatment Plan for I-4 Nx:
(1966 Revision)

1. <u>Goals</u>. Long-range goals include: elimination of delinquency; reduction or resolution of internal conflicts; reduction of fear of own needs and impulses, and of use of defense mechanisms in harmful ways (to self or others); changed self-image in direction of capacity for enjoyment and happiness (personal, interpersonal), sense of personal worth and of potential worth (as a mature person) to others; greater awareness of actual (vs. imaginary) strengths and limitations, needs and impulses; more accurate perception of who he is and really wants to be, in contrast to perception of self in terms of definitions and roles he has gotten or accepted from others for reasons of security and defense, or partial and indirect gratification; increased feeling of the legitimacy of his own needs and of desires for self-fulfillment in reality; movement toward I-5 (increased perceptual differentiation of self and others, increased self knowledge, increased awareness of complex patterns in others); increased level of functioning (improved role definitions) in school, job, family and other relevant areas. Short-term (immediate) goals include: establishment of treatment contract between NX and Treatment Agent or between family and Agent; moratorium on acting-out behavior; specified and agreed-upon plan regarding initial placement, job, school, etc.

2. <u>Placement Plan</u>. Place NX at home initially if parents are willing to accept his or her return and if

the NX is willing. Placement at home is essential if family group therapy (conjoint family therapy) is the treatment of choice. If Nx's own family is unavailable or if they are unable or unwilling to modify problem-producing interactions, Nx may be placed in foster or group home temporarily or permanently. Real emancipation from the home can only begin when the Nx himself recognizes that this is the only (or best) solution. Characteristics of a out-of-home placement appropriate for the Nx are: home provides a base from which Nx can work on resolution of internal conflicts, emancipation and identity problems; home allows the Nx some independence: parents can relate flexibly to the Nx on a closeness-distance dimension; parents can permit the Nx to take the initiative in determining their relationship; parents must be tolerant, accepting and non-threatening; parents must be permissive regarding Nx's continued relationships with his own family; and parents should be able to communicate to the Treatment Agent significant cues regarding the Nx's emotional state.

3. Family Treatment. Formal family group therapy (conjoint family therapy) should be treatment of choice if: (a) mother and father figures and other relevant family members are available; (b) all family members agree to the treatment; and (c) individual contacts between the Nx and Agent are unnecessary. Under these conditions, the family accepts the responsibility for the Nx as with any other family member; i.e., responsibility for decisions regarding job, school, and behavior. Less formal family treatment (family conferences) can occur without the above conditions being met. In the latter instance, individual and group methods should also be used, and the goal may be emancipation from the home. Family treatment may facilitate the emancipation process. Since

the Nx may try to re-enact his family problem in a foster or group home setting, the Agent should offer support to the substitute parents via understanding and suggested techniques for dealing with Nx.

4. <u>Location of Community Supports</u>. Typically, not relevant to the Nx's delinquency problem at intake. Agent may get information for the Nx and encourage participation in community activities as treatment progresses .

5. <u>School and Job Recommendations</u>. With the Nx, the first problem to be solved relates to the neurotic aspects of the delinquency; therefore, school or job is a secondary issue. The significance of these activities as aspects of the initial plan varies from Nx to Nx. School and job requirements may be control issues relevant to the initial phases of treatment. These factors become more important in their own right in the development of individual potential as treatment progresses.

6. <u>Leisure Time Activities</u>. Project-sponsored activities may be used as a supplement to specific treatment methods. Offer constructive activities which will satisfy the individual Nx and which will meet his status needs in terms of the standards of the larger culture.

7. <u>Peer Group Variables</u>. If an individual Nx plan is based on individual psychotherapy primarily, he or she may be encouraged to participate with a peer group of I-4's in social activities in order to increase fund of interpersonal skills and satisfactions. Nx's may be asked to assist with lower maturity subtypes as a means of enhancing the Nx's ego identity and sense of value to others.

8. 8. <u>Kind of Controls</u>. Major focus is on internal, psychological controls. Nx should be encouraged to develop and use appropriate inner controls. Some external controls may be necessary initially. Issues of control may be used therapeutically by the Agent for purposes of communicating support and concern. Nx may raise issues relating to trust, personal acceptance, the impact of own impulses or counter dependency by deliberately challenging Agent's rules or personal standards (stated or unstated). Areas of conflict between the Nx and the Agent should be carefully chosen so that the Nx may sometimes "win the argument" without being lost to the program. The content of the issues should be real and important to both the Nx and the Agent, nevertheless.

9. <u>Kind of Agent</u>. Agent should be internally-oriented and comfortable with identity as a treator. He should not fear emotional disturbance and should have understanding of and respect for neurotic and coping defenses. He should have considerable self-knowledge regarding dynamics and be able to handle issues of transference and countertransference. He should be willing to make himself open (emotionally available) to the Nx, so that two-way communication on a feeling level is possible. Under some conditions, the Agent may be able to serve as an identity model for Nx. The Agent should be an individual of personality complexity, one who has resolved or greatly reduced any major personal problems. If the Agent has not experienced personal difficulties in his own life, he may be less sensitive to the intensity of the Nx's feelings, his needs and his limitations.

10. <u>Treatment Methods</u>. Major methods are individual psychotherapy, group psychotherapy and/or family group therapy (conjoint family therapy), with an emphasis

on the development of insight into conflicts, personal capacities and family problems. Activity groups, school tutoring and environmental manipulation may be used as appropriate in line with overall goals.

11. <u>Suggested Techniques for Achieving Goals</u>. Encourage the Nx to explore the environment and, at the same time, permit him to experience the consequences of these exploratory actions. Provide him with opportunities to practice a variety of social roles, to "try them on for size." Allow the Nx time to integrate roles and choices with other aspects of his overall adjustment pattern - his areas of actual strength and limitations, his emerging picture of himself and of his changing standards and ideals. Regardless of the type of psychotherapy, timing and level of interpretation are very important - with decisions to be made on the basis of Nx's ego strength, consciousness of conflicts, etc. Focus on symptoms (delinquency) is useless or worse; Agent should concentrate on underlying feelings and problems. Considerable emotional support for the Nx should be forthcoming from the Agent, group or family while conflicts are being resolved, particularly during crises. The Agent should be aware of and openly label support available for the Nx from the family and the peer group, as well as from the Nx for the family and peer group.

12. <u>Kind of Help the Agent Needs</u>. Consultation and supervision regarding dynamics of cases, and counter transference reactions, is essential. Agent needs a source of support for continual reevaluation of self in a treator role; assistance in continually evaluating the Nx's potential for growth, the Agent's level of interpretations, timing, etc. Training and consultation are needed regarding the specific treatment methods being applied.

13. <u>Questions</u>. A small percentage of Nxs are so emotionally disturbed as to be better treated in a residential setting. How can these individuals be identified and eliminated from community programs?

Chapter 7

Concluding Remarks

My Introduction pretty well explains the purpose of the book.
There are certain, identifiable personality types that are not
generally understood and consequently do not receive appropriate
treatment. As a consequence, the very behavior which is desired to
be extinguished is reinforced.

One of the primary goals of the I-Level Theory was to recognize
these personality differences and to develop differential treatment
methods that would meet the specific needs of each type. The I-Level
Theory not only identified the different personality types, but it also
suggested possible treatment methods. As stated in the 1966 edition
of the I-Level Theory paper, "...the scheme can now be regarded as
one which has withstood an operational test in the field." However, in
his introduction to the I-Level theory, Cal Terhune, Superintendent
of O.H. Close School stated "...it will undoubtedly be revised in the
light of continued experiences."

At O.H. Close, we increased our experiences by incorporating
portions of other theories. Each of these other theories contributed
to the treatment methods employed as well as the success rate.

We employed principles of Transactional Analysis, Gestalt Therapy, Operant Conditioning and Sensory Stimulation as well as the principles of The Therapeutic Community, Time Structuring, Relationship Building, Counseling (Individual and Small Group), and Community Meetings. By integrating these various concepts into a generalized Basic Plan, we were able to implement a treatment program that was able to effectively treat a variety of personalities requiring specific, individualized techniques.

The basic concepts described were tested in a variety of environments. Diagnosis coupled with the prescribed treatment for that specific personality, repeatedly proved to be successful in achieving our goal—that of helping dysfunctional persons become functional, within their capacity. The youths were evaluated every two months by a treatment team of ten members. Their treatment goals were established at their first case conference by having the youth describe what he would like to change about himself while incarcerated.

Though each of our youths had different backgrounds, different intellects, different educations and different goals, after six to eight months in our treatment program, they all seemed ready to return to the community as productive members. The differences between their backgrounds and their common results, in the same time frame, was difficult to explain.

In an effort to measure their rate of change, in relation to their involvement in the basic treatment plan, we discovered a common denominator that all the youths demonstrated.

There was an inverse relationship between their involvement in the basic plan and their aggressive attitude and behavior. The more they worked on the 10 points, the less aggressive they were.

I can only speculate on the significance of this phenomena. I was seeking one answer and completely overlooked the more obvious one. It wasn't until I was working on this book that I suddenly recognized this reality. This raised the question: "Were we extinguishing aggression or reinforcing amiability, or both?" Perhaps the best explanation is Skinner's statement: "Two ways of effectively preventing unwanted conditioned behavior are: to (1) extinguish it by withholding reinforcement and (2) to condition some incompatible behavior."

At this stage, I'm no longer in a position to explore this phenomenon more thoroughly. However, I know this: wherever the methods described in this book were applied, that unit had the lowest recidivism rate of any other unit in the state of California, as reported by the CYA parole division.

PERMISSIONS

The author wishes to thank the following publishers and organizations for granting permission for the extensive reprinting and quoting of source material that was so necessary and so intrinsic to the compilation of my book and to its central argument. While the quoting may be deemed excessive, my vision for *Troubled to Treasured. Strong Willed Child or Strong Willed Parent?* was that of a reference guide, to ultimately make as clear and as accessible as possible the key concepts I wished to convey about truly successful treatment strategies for delinquent youth.

The idea was to build a formidable theoretical frame from some of the greatest minds in the field and demonstrate how my experiences both supported and challenged some assumptions. Paraphrasing these great minds and their work was simply not an option, given the complexity of the material. Therefore, the author begs forgiveness for such unusually lengthy and oft-quoted passages, and gratefully acknowledges the generous permissions granted with regard to the works of Skinner, Yontef and Berne.

My thanks to Joe Wysong of the Gestalt Journal Press for permission to extensively quote Gary Yontef, from Dialogue, ...

My thanks to Random House Inc. for permission to quote from Berne's *Transactional Analysis in Psychotherapy,* 1961.

My thanks to McGraw Hill for permission to quote from *The Analysis of Behavior: A Program for Self-Instruction.*

Sources of References Cited

Books

Berne, E. (1961). *Transactional Analysis In Psychotherapy*. New York: Grove Press Inc.

Berne, E. (1964). *Games People Play*. New York: Grove Press Inc.

Holland, J. G. & Skinner, B.F. (1961). *The Analysis of Behavior: A Program for Self Instruction*. New York: McGraw-Hill Book Co., Inc.

Perls, F. S. (1969). *Gestalt Therapy Verbatim*. Lafayette, CA: Real People Press.

Perls, F. S. (1969). *In and Out of the Garbage Pail*. Lafayette, CA: Real People Press.

Redl, F. & Wineman, D. (1957). *The Aggressive Child*. Glencoe, Illinois: The Free Press.

Yontef, G. (1993). *Awareness, Dialogue, and Process*. Gouldsboro, ME: Gestalt Journal Press.

Zubek, J. (Ed.). (1969). *Sensory Deprivation. Fifteen Years of Research.* New York: Appleton Century Crofts.

Journals, Reports and Other Publications

California Youth Authority: 1965. *Interpersonal Maturity Level Classification: Juvenile Diagnosis and Treatment of Low, Middle and High Maturity Delinquents.* Warren, M. Q.; The Community Treatment Staff, Community Treatment Project.

California Youth Authority: 1966. *Interpersonal Maturity Level Classification: Juvenile Diagnosis and Treatment of Low, Middle and High Maturity Delinquents.* Warren, M. Q.; The Community Treatment Staff, Community Treatment Project.

Sullivan, C., Grant, M. Q., & Grant, D. J. (1957) The Development of Interpersonal Maturity: Applications to Delinquency. *Psychiatry, 20,* 373-385.